IRISH WOMEN'S
LETTERS

This book is dedicated to all Irish women,
Ancient and Modern,
from the very first Mesolithic woman
who stepped on Ireland's shore
8,000 years ago.
But particularly to two Irish women
especially dear to me: My first wife, Deirdre,
who died in March 1984 and my second wife, Eileen,
who died in November 1998

IRISH WOMEN'S LETTERS

Compiled by
LAURENCE FLANAGAN

Foreword by
EDNA O'BRIEN

SUTTON PUBLISHING

First published in 1997 by
Sutton Publishing Limited · Phoenix Mill
Thrupp · Stroud · Gloucestershire · GL5 2BU

Paperback edition first published in 1999

British Library Cataloguing in Publication Data
A catalogue record for this book is available from the British Library.

ISBN 0 7509 2219 2

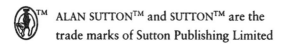

™ ALAN SUTTON™ and SUTTON™ are the
trade marks of Sutton Publishing Limited

Typeset in 10/15pt Sabon.
Typesetting and origination by
Sutton Publishing Limited.
Printed in Great Britain by
The Guernsey Press Company Limited,
Guernsey, Channel Islands.

CONTENTS

CONTENTS

CONTENTS

CONTENTS

CONTENTS

CONTENTS

Note by Compiler

The letters in this selection have been chosen to cover as wide a range, both chronologically and thematically, as possible. The rule has been that no correspondent was allowed more than two pieces to the same addressee. All the pieces have been previously published, which should make access to additional material by the same author easier. The chronological ordering has been based on the date of the first letter of each writer. Very few of those letters published in 'Calendars' of documents are printed word for word; the great majority appear in précis form, giving the subject of the letter.

FOREWORD

Two things in particular strike me about these letters – the enduring spirit of these women and their sense of being excluded from the seat of power.

The rich, the poor, the holy, the infamous and even the brave seem at all times to be appealing to a higher echelon of authority and this whether it be a genteel widow pleading with the Lord Lieutenant for her husband's pension not to be discontinued or an abandoned wife telling a truant husband that her chattels are being sold to pay his debts or a defiant Constance Markievicz chafing about her English captors. Hers are the most moving in the entire collection simply because they convey her dauntless and witty spirit. By comparison Maria Edgeworth and Charlotte Brontë while being entertaining are more self-conscious, mindful of their role as great writers. Emily Brontë on the other hand permits herself a word which would send our puny modern 'critics' into a lather. She describes a morning as 'divinic'.

What is so compelling about almost all the letters is the precise rendering of time, place and the emotional circumstances in which they were written. For instance, poor Mary Cumming's account of being sea-sick, nursed by a loving husband and only able to swallow a sip of port wine and water, is deeply moving. She goes on to delight us with the marvels of the New World and then crushes us with the death of her infant child. Happiness, tragedy; the several lives charted with a precision that any historian might envy. All the letters bear witness to that wry paradox of women's inner strength and resilence in contrast with a more manifest male sovereignty.

If I have any reservation it is that I would like more, many more.

Edna O'Brien

INTRODUCTION

One of the first problems to be faced in compiling a selection of letters by Irish women is, quite simply, how do we define 'being Irish'?

In the case of many of those selected, the answer is refreshingly simple. Saint Bríd was born in Ireland of Irish parents; Nora Joyce was born in Ireland of Irish parents; Kitty Kiernan was born in Ireland of Irish parents; Mary Cumming was born in Ireland of Irish parents. These, without fear of contradiction, we can accept as Irish. In similar vein, Helen Waddell was born in Tokyo – but of Irish parents; Constance, Countess Markievicz, was born in London, but of Irish parents; Edith Somerville was born in Corfu, but of Irish parents. We can hardly deny these ladies their Irishness. What then of the Brontës? Although born in Yorkshire, their father was unquestionably Irish, and was even christened Patrick as a result of having been born on St Patrick's Day. Few, if any, authorities would describe the Brontë sisters as 'Irish writers', but they certainly have a claim to be described as Irish women. Maud Gonne, on the other hand, was born in Aldershot, the daughter of a British army officer, and came to Ireland only when her father's regiment was posted to Dublin in 1882. This seems, at first sight, the very antithesis of any claim to 'Irishness'. Yet she became – and with incredible speed – as anti-English as possible, identifying herself totally with the evicted, the dispossessed: she became, in short, like so many English men and women, 'more Irish than the Irish'. And yet it was not until 1903, when she married Major John MacBride, former commander of the so-called 'Irish Brigade' in the Boer War, that she became legally Irish. The same, of course, is true of Mary Delany, whose marriage in 1743 to Patrick Delany made her legally Irish.

These two marriages of English women to Irish men – though to Irish men of totally different outlooks, the one a dedicated Nationalist whose sincerity was enshrined in his execution, the other a cleric of the Church of Ireland whose unrelenting flattery of the viceroy sacrificed his friendship with Swift – reminds us that while in person-to-person situations the Irish and the English can survive in amity, such amity was in short supply from the first arrival of Anglo-Norman conquerors in Ireland in 1167, as far as the interests of the two nations were concerned. The arrival of the Anglo-Normans, or 'Franks', as the Irish annalists called them, created one major new element in Irish society – what, in effect, amounted to the establishment of a kind of civil service, so that official documents were stored centrally. That this civil service eventually led to the establishment of a secret service was something of a natural progression.

Three particular instances of strained relations between the Irish and the English government concern us in reading these letters by Irish women. The first of these was the events leading up to the Rebellion of 1798. The Irish parliament was not a very satisfactory institution, and the manner of its election fell far short of the democratic ideal. The major part of the population – the Roman Catholics – was not represented. They were not allowed to vote. Parliament's reluctance to reform itself led to widespread dissatisfaction: not, surprisingly, among the disenfranchised, but, at the outset, among Ulster Protestants. It was in Belfast that the Society of United Irishmen was first launched in 1791, by Samuel McTier and Robert Simms. Initially the society aimed to secure a measure of parliamentary reform and for several years pursued this goal by constitutional means. A branch was formed in Dublin by Wolfe Tone and Thomas Russell in the hope of uniting all Irishmen in the pursuit of universal male suffrage. In 1794 the Dublin society was proscribed and inevitably, driven underground. It then became a secret, oath-bound, elaborately organized and centrally directed body, now Republican in outlook and intent on the separation of the two kingdoms. Attempts were made to enlist the active support of the French government. The authorities employed brutal methods in their attempts to suppress the society, references to which will be found in the letters of Mary Ann McCracken. In 1798 uprisings took place in different parts of the country, and many names appeared to take honourable places in the pages of Irish history. In Wexford, while many

Protestants did join the insurgents, the insurrection sadly degenerated into sectarian conflict and was put down with a ruthlessness that made heroes out of such as Fr John Murphy of Boolavogue, who was brutally flogged, beheaded and burnt in pitch. In Ulster the insurgents were mainly Presbyterian by religion and Republican in politics. After the rout of the battle of Antrim Henry Joy McCracken, a member of the Society of United Irishmen, escaped briefly, was captured and subsequently publicly hanged in his native Belfast. In Mayo inadequate French forces landed in Killala Bay, initially meeting with some success – in the Castlebar Races a large contingent of British forces was ignominiously defeated, but soon afterwards the French and their Irish supporters were defeated at Ballinamuck. The defeat of the insurgents was followed by massacre and indiscriminate killings and, in 1800, by the Act of Union, which instead of reforming the Irish parliament, abolished it.

The second example of Irish discontent with British rule is touched upon, but rather tangentially, by the relationship of Lady Jane Francesca Wilde to the voice of the Young Ireland group, *The Nation*. She wrote for it under the pseudonym 'Speranza' until the imprisonment of John Gavan Duffy in 1848, when she replaced him as leader-writer. Young Ireland was the vehicle by which a kind of romantic nationalism entered Irish politics, with a large amount of intellectual input by people such as Thomas Davis. It led to neither insurrection nor rebellion but fizzled out with only a confrontation with police at Ballingarry, Co. Tipperary, subsequently referred to as 'the battle of the widow McCormick's cabbage patch'.

The third example of Irish discontent with British rule to confront us is, of course, the Irish Rebellion of 1916, as a result of which one of our correspondents, Constance Countess Markievicz, was imprisoned, while another, Maud Gonne MacBride, lost her husband, Major John MacBride, who was executed for his part in the Rebellion (he was one of the commanders at Jacob's Mill). Briefly, the Rebellion, or 'Rising' as it is also termed, was a failure; most of its leaders were executed. The harshness of its repression was an even greater failure, leading, as it did, to a wave of revulsion, to a more united attitude to Nationalist politics and, ultimately, to the 'War of Independence'. The proclamation read by Patrick Pearse, 'In the name of God and of the dead generations from which she receives her old tradition of nationhood, Ireland, through us, summons her children to her flag and strikes for her freedom', summed up the aspirations to be fought for in the War of Independence in which Mícheál Collins played a significant, even indispensable, role. Unfortunately, the War of Independence was followed inevitably by civil war between 1922 and 1923, in which Mícheál Collins again played a prominent role as Commander of the Free State forces (i.e. those who had accepted the Anglo-Irish Treaty).

It is not surprising, perhaps, that such differences of opinion between the Irish and the British government led to immediate, and sustained, increases in the numbers of Irish emigrants. This was not always voluntary. After the rebellion of 1798 considerable numbers of those *believed* to have been involved were transported as convicts, but to a new destination – Australia, and particularly New South Wales; the war between Britain and America in 1776 had meant that America was no longer available as a destination for transported convicts. Between 1800 and 1803 New South Wales was the destination of some 942 Irish convicts, 715 of whom were supposed to have been United Irishmen. Between 1792 and 1868 a total of some 28,000 Irish were transported to New South Wales, Van Diemen's Land and Western Australia. In the 1850s some 100,000 immigrants also went – a fair number probably attracted by the discovery of gold in 1851. Meanwhile, of course, 'voluntary' emigration to America continued, if 'voluntary' can be used to describe attempts to find a famine-free life; in 1851, for example, a peak of a quarter of a million left Ireland for America. Obviously Mary Cumming's transatlantic move was very different from the antipodean journeys of Biddy Burke or Isabella Wyly – or at least the reasons for it were very different. All the letters do, however, give fascinating glimpses of the problems encountered far from home and Ireland.

These letters from far away do not, surprisingly, reveal a shatteringly wide gulf between the literary achievements of a relatively well-educated middle-class girl like Mary Cumming, whose father was a minister, and a girl like Biddy Burke whose father was admittedly a well-to-do farmer, but in an area which was still largely Irish-speaking as late as 1880. Bearing this in mind, Biddy's letter is remarkably well-turned.

Humour is seldom far distant from Irish writing of any kind and it is refreshing to discover that even in prison, in exile, in Aylesbury, Constance Gore-Booth (the Countess Markievicz) maintained her sense of it, as expressed in her signature. This totally natural humour is not very different from that of Charlotte Frances Shaw's description of her husband's visit to the front, or Violet Florence Martin's description of her rather hilarious journey to the Currarevagh Ball. To compensate for the humour – even, in a way to validate it – we have a portion of pathos. The mature, but touching, letter of Edith Somerville describing her mother's death is a dignified sister to Mary Cumming's account of the death of her child. Indignation is, perhaps, a more common human emotion; while Constance Mary Wilde's indignation at the treatment of her husband is controlled and remarkably dignified also, that of her mother-in-law, regarding the court case involving Mary Travers, is delightfully real – even bitchy.

Family life, with its ups and downs, is a regular theme: the letters of both Anne and Emily Brontë read almost like school reports, while Lily Yeats enjoys a moan in one letter and in the other, in addition to a whimsical allusion to her brother's most famous poem, engages in speculation about family history. More importantly, she reveals interesting sidelights on the attitudes of some landlords to the famine. Inevitably the emigrants' letters are full of information about families. Since marriage is the foundation of most families it is a recurrent theme among these letters, not only in the rather bizarre petition of Katherine Fitzgerald and the 'imaginary' letters of Maria Edgeworth, from her epistolary novels *Leonora* and *Letters of Julia and Caroline*, but in snatches in letters by Lady Francesca Wilde and Charlotte Frances Shaw. Since many marriages contain at least a germ of love it is not surprising to find this theme well represented in letters by Nora Joyce and, of course, Kitty Kiernan.

Monastic celibacy is, of course, the direct antithesis of marriage. In the early Irish Church many thousands of pious men and women devoted their lives to the service of God after the introduction of Christianity by Saint Patrick in about AD 432. Of many of these 'saints', or holy men and women, we know very little. Of some, however, we know a great deal, though much information must have been destroyed not only in the incursions of the Vikings but also at the Dissolution of the Monasteries. While a letter from the hand of St Patrick survives, the famous 'Letter to the Soldiers of Coroticus', it is unfortunate that the letter from Bríd to St Aid disappeared, more by carelessness than anything else, some thousand years after her death.

In conclusion, it seems appropriate to quote what is not a letter, but a recorded conversation between Queen Medb (Maeve) and her husband Ailill, taken from the version of 'Táin Bó Cúalnge' contained in the *Book of Leinster*, and known as the 'pillow talk'. It is a fair statement of a woman's pride in her situation.

For that reason my father gave me one of the provinces of Ireland, namely, the province of Crúachu. Whence I am called Medb Chrúachna. Messengers came from Find mac Rosa Rúaid, the King of Leinster, to sue for me, and from Cairbre Nia Fermac Rosa, the King of Tara, and they came from Conchobor mac Fachtna, the King of Ulster, and they came from Eochu Bec. But I consented not, for I demanded a strange bride-gift such as no woman before me had asked of a man of the men of Ireland, to wit, a husband without meanness, without jealousy, without fear. If my husband should be mean, it would not be fitting for us to be together, for I am generous in largesse and the bestowal of gifts and it would be a reproach for my husband that I should be better than he in generosity, but it would be no reproach if we were equally generous provided that both of us were generous. If my husband were timorous, neither would it be fitting for us to be together, for single-handed I am victorious in battles and contests and combat, and it would be a reproach for my husband that his wife should be more courageous than he, but it is no reproach if they are equally courageous provided that both are courageous. If the man with whom I should be were jealous, neither would it be fitting, for I was never without one lover quickly succeeding another. Now such a husband have I got, even you, Ailill mac Rosa Rúaid of Leinster. You are not niggardly, you are not jealous, you are not inactive.

MEDIEVAL

The medieval period in Ireland – stretching as it did from the introduction of Christianity in the fifth century and including the arrival of the Anglo-Normans, or Franks, in 1167 – saw a great deal of activity in this island: military, political, social, economic, ecclesiastical and literary. The hundreds of religious cells founded in the early phases of Christianity, some of which grew to become famous international centres of learning, have left sometimes scanty, sometimes stupendous, records of their former glory. But the vicissitudes they suffered were spectacular. Clonmacnoise, Co. Offaly, for example, founded on 25 February 547, by Saint Ciaran, grew to be a great monastery, with an impressive product-list attached to its scriptoria, and one equally impressive attached to its workshops. However, in the course of its glorious history, it was ravaged by fire thirteen times between 722 and 1205; it was plundered by the Vikings eight times between 832 and 1163; it was attacked by Irish enemies twenty-seven times between 832 and 1163; it was plundered by the English six times between 1178 and 1204. Finally, in 1552 it was reduced to total ruin by the English from Athlone so that 'not a bell, large or small, or an image, or an altar, or a book, or a gem, or even glass in a window was left which was not carried away'. It is amazing, in the light of such histories, that any documents survive from this period. It makes it even more ironic that the letter of St Bríd, or at least a copy of it, should have survived only to be lost in seventeenth-century Belgium.

The establishment of what amounted to a sort of civil service, by the Anglo-Normans from the twelfth century onwards, with official documents stored centrally, did, however, ensure that these documents, or at least a major portion of them, were preserved, does enable us to admire the formidable Rohesia de Verdun and to sympathize with her predicaments. Because these later medieval documents were official, and therefore preserved, they tend on the one hand to concentrate on the problems of the Anglo-Norman gentry and on the other to concentrate on legal matters, especially those where the intervention of the King was either necessary or was seen to be beneficial. Very few are in the names of women – possibly as few as one in a thousand. Those that have survived show that there were some remarkable women in medieval Ireland. The castle-building Rohesia seems to have had much in common with Máirgrég (Margaret), the wife of Calbach Úa Conchobuir, who hosted a great traditional feasting of court poets and historians at Killeigh, Co. Offaly, in 1451. She goes down in Irish history as the only woman interested 'in preparing highways and erecting bridges and churches'.

Saint Bríd (Brigid, Bridget)

St Bríd was born in the mid-fifth century, probably in Co. Kildare, both her parents being of noble Leinster stock, both apparently Christians. There is, however, a strong tradition in Co. Louth that she was born in Faughart, near Dundalk. In her childhood Bríd displayed conspicuous generosity to the poor and needy; on one occasion her generosity seriously depleted her mother's supply of butter. Conscious that her mother was about to take stock, and the depletion to be revealed, young Bríd prayed to God and the supply of butter was miraculously restored. A bishop called Macaille, who lived near her parents' home, is credited with clothing Bríd in the white cloak and veil characteristic of the holy women of the time. It seems likely that her first convent was at Kildare, on a piece of ground given her by the King of Leinster, and marked by a large oak-tree, which gave its name to the convent – 'Church of the Oak-tree'. It seems likely too that it was on the site of a pagan sanctuary, some of whose traditions were preserved: a perpetual fire, tended by nineteen nuns, for example, was maintained there until the dissolution. Bríd is credited with many miracles, among them curing the sick, especially lepers. There is a story that on one occasion she was tending a dying pagan chief; she spent the time praying and plaiting a cross from the rushes on the floor. The chief opened his eyes and asked what she was doing, so she explained to him the significance of the cross; he was so impressed that he asked to be baptized before he died. From this incident arose the practice of plaiting St Brigid's Crosses. She is known as 'The Prophetess of Christ, the Queen of the South, the Mary of the Gael'. There is a multitude of churches, ancient and modern, throughout Ireland, dedicated to her. Accounts of her life exist in quantity, the earliest in Irish or Latin, later ones in French, German and Flemish. She herself is credited with the composition of several works, including 'A Rule for the Nuns of her Foundation', a poem on the virtues of St Patrick and 'The Quiver of Divine Love, or the Desires of the Faithful'. She died in about 524 and there is a tradition that she is buried at Downpatrick, Co. Down, along with Patrick and Colmcille.

THE EARLIEST IRISH WOMAN'S LETTER

In addition to the works listed above Bríd is credited with an epistle, or letter, to St Aid, son of Degill. This was in the possession of John Colgan, who was engaged in the editing and compilation of a great mass of Irish manuscripts, mainly relating to Irish ecclesiastical history, in the seventeenth century, at Louvain in Belgium. At his death in 1658 many of the manuscripts disappeared, including Bríd's letter. We know, however, from a note of Colgan's, that it was in a kind of Irish rhyme, and in it she was dissuading St Aid from setting off on a journey.

However our *Bridgid* writ

A Rule for the Nuns of her own Foundation.

An Epistle to St. Aid, the Son of Degill, in a kind of Irish Rhime, therein dissuading him from travelling.

A Poem on the Vertues of St. Patrick.

The Quiver of Divine Love, or the Desires of the faithful.

[*Colgan J* affirms, that the three last of these Pieces, written in the *Irish* Language, were in his Possession.]

Sir Richard Ware, *The History and Antiquities of Ireland, with the History of the Writers of Ireland*, translated by Walter Harris, Robert Bell, Dublin (1784)

Rohesia de Verdun

Rohesia de Verdun was daughter of, and heir to, Nicholas de Verdun and grand-daughter of Bertram de Verdun to whom the site of Dundalk, Co. Louth, had been granted in 1186. She was obviously a formidable lady, writing to Henry III on several occasions. That she was, in every respect, formidable is shown by the fact that in 1236 she fortified a castle in her own land, against the native Irish, 'which none of her predecessors was able to do'; she proposed to raise another castle near the sea, 'for the greater security of the King's land'. So impressed was the king that he granted her the King's service of Meath and Uriel for forty days for this purpose.

A Shrewd Deal

In order to ensure her inheritance, and to avoid any threat of an unwanted marriage, Rohesia made a deal with Henry, in October 1231; in April of the following year the king instructed Maurice FitzGerald, justiciary of Ireland, to grant her request.

Rohesia, daughter and heir of Nicholas de Verdun, made with the K. a fine of 700 marks for her relief, that she may have seisin of her father's lands at his death which belong to her by right of inheritance, and that she may not be constrained to marry. The K. has taken her homage. Mandate to the sheriffs of Warwick and Leicester to cause her to have seisin of all the lands of her inheritance within their bailiwicks.

Legal Action

In May, 1233, Rohesia took legal action to protect part of her property.

Rohesia de Verdun attorns Robert de Everdon and Richard de Wuditon against Robert le Mor, plaintiff, and Richard de Fold, tenant, who calls Rohesia to warranty, of 2 carucates of land in Ricardefeld; against Henry Durant, plaintiff, of 1 carucate in the same vill, whereof Richard calls Rohesia to warranty; against Richard de Tavernac, plaintiff, of a moiety of a lake in Balibandric, whereof Richard de Molendino calls Rohesia to warranty; and against Denis Bagot, plaintiff, of the third part of 2½ carucates in Raz, held by Rohesia.

Further Legal Action

Unfortunately Rohesia had to take further legal action in April 1238 – a formidable adversary indeed. However, on her death in 1246 the king instructed John FitzGeoffrey, justiciary of Ireland, to take into the king's hands

'all the lands and tenements which belonged to Rohesia de Verdun, deceased',
so that in May 1247 her son John had to start the process all over again.

Rohesia de Verdun, tenant, attorns Robert de Werston and William de St. German against Robert de Braybuef and Margery, his wife, plaintiffs, of 3 carucates of land in Glummore and Aydevalan.

The said Rohesia, tenant, attorns John de Wudeton and Henry de Wutton, against John de Nutreville, plaintiff, of 14 acres of land in Octerath.

ed. H.S. Sweetman, *Calendar of Documents Relating to Ireland,*
1171–1251, Longman, London (1875)

Amicia de Lucy

A micia de Lucy was the wife of William de Lucy and finds herself constrained to take legal action to obtain her rights.

A LADY IN LEGAL DIFFICULTIES

It is not recorded to whom Amicia's letter of July 1251 was addressed; it
may have been to the king or one of his officers.

Amicia, who was the wife of William de Lucy, puts in her place Philip de Lucy and William of Kilfeacle, clerk, or either of them, in her plea to prosecute in Ireland a writ of dower *Unde nihil habet* against Philip Keling, Robert le Flemeng, Simon Serle, and Henry of Balimalidan.

ed. H.S. Sweetman, *Calendar of Documents Relating to Ireland,*
1171–1251, Longman, London (1875)

Mariota, Prioress of Clonard

S t Mary's Abbey of Augustinian nuns was founded by O'Melaghlin, ruler of Meath, in 1144, and was almost certainly the first of the houses of Irish nuns to be established under the influence of St Malachy, as it ranked as the head house of the Arroasian canonesses in Ireland until after 1195.

THE RESIGNATION OF AN ABBESS

In 1288 the prioress and convent experienced a great difficulty through the rather abrupt resignation of Borgenilda, their recently elected abbess. In June of that year, therefore, the prioress wrote to the king invoking his assistance.

Their monastery being vacant by the resignation of Borgenilda, lately elected abbess, pray for licence to elect. Send Brother John, canon of the house of St. Peter of Clonard, bearer of these presents, to obtain this licence; and further urgently pray the K. that in order to spare them labour and expense he will command his escheator of Ireland to receive fealty in lieu of the K. from the elect, and on confirmation to restore their small temporalities, of special grace.
Clonard.

A FURTHER PLEA TO THE KING

In September of 1288 Mariota, prioress of the convent again writes to the king for assistance. The request is subsequently answered, for in October the king writes to John, Archbishop of Dublin, acting as justiciary of Ireland, requesting that he restore the temporalities, 'having first received from the elect letters under her seal and that of the chapter that this grant shall not tend to the King's prejudice or disherison'.

Their convent having become vacant, they had by the K.'s licence elected their sister, the Lady Burgenylda, as abbess of their house. Wherefore they send Brother Robert, canon of the house of St. Mary of Navan, in the diocese of Meath, praying the K.'s grace and the royal assent. They further pray that the K. will command the justiciary to restore the temporalities when the election shall have been confirmed.

ed. H.S. Sweetman, *Calendar of Documents Relating to Ireland, 1285–1292*, Longman, London (1879)

TUDOR

The first of these reigns affected Ireland most strongly by the Dissolution of the Monasteries, and the consequent destruction of much documentation, as well, of course, as the destruction of the fabric of the buildings themselves. Poor Mariota's Cell of Clonard, consisting of a church with gardens and 62 acres of land, was valued in 1540 at 40 shillings and leased to Gerald FitzGerald. Other bigger and greater establishments suffered similar fates: the great Cistercian monastery of Mellifont was possessed of 5,000 acres, several granges, five water-mills and many fisheries and boats in 1540, in 1566 the dissolved monastery was occupied by Edward More. The Abbey of St Thomas the Martyr in Dublin was possessed of at least 2,300 acres of land; the site of this monastery was granted to William Brabazon in 1545. So much land suddenly made available was a certain vehicle for contention, and an even more certain one was the recurring reluctance of monarchs to pay for services rendered. (It was a tendency of Henry VIII to avoid paying bills if he could; in 1526 the gun-foundry in Mechelen, which had cast the famous 'Twelve Apostles', ceased supplying the king because of his failure to pay bills.)

Elizabeth was probably no less reluctant to settle debts than her father had been. Her experience of Ireland was probably more exciting, however. Apart from an occasional rebellion, such as that in Munster which had Ursula, Lady St Leger, justifiably worried about her own safety, she had to face the threat of the mighty Armada, sent by Philip II of Spain in 1588, and the all too real possibility of many thousands of heavily armed Spanish soldiers rampant in Ireland. In the light of this daunting menace the activities of the pirate queen, Gráinne ní Mhaille, were probably viewed with great concern five years later. The preservation of a simple heart-felt plea from Katherin Eggarton to her husband is almost certainly due to its having been referred to Lord Burghley.

Anne, Lady Skeffyngton

Lady Skeffyngton was the widow of Sir William Skeffyngton, who had been Lord Deputy until his death on 31 December 1535. She had written to the queen, Henry VIII's second wife, Anne Boleyn, asking her for assistance.

A PLEA FOR JUSTICE

After writing to Anne Boleyn, Lady Skeffyngton wrote, on 26 January, from Dublin, to Thomas Cromwell, or Crumwell, who was a member of the Council of Ireland.

Her husband, Sir William, died Dec. 31. Without the King's pity she and all her children are utterly undone. Desires to be allowed her petition.

THE PETITION

With her letter to Cromwell she included a petition, to be shown to Mr Secretary.

Articles of petition for Anne Lady Skeffyngton, to be shown to Mr Secretary: – To be allowed the stipend due to her late husband as well in England as in Ireland. Four teams of great cart horses. Desires to be transported home, with servants.

FURTHER DIFFICULTIES

On 18 February she was obliged to write again to Thomas Cromwell.

Complains of being greatly troubled, vexed, and hindered many ways by Lord Leonard Gray, who detained her goods, intercepted her letters to the King and him, and arrested the ships she had hired.

A PLEA FOR MONEY DUE AND PARDON FOR DEBTS

On 10 January of the following year, 1537, poor Anne was still in difficulty. Again she wrote to Thomas Cromwell.

Her suit for money due from the King to her late husband for certain matters in Ireland. Beseeches him to procure from the King her pardon for certain debts owing by her late husband, there being proclamations and writs of outlawry issued against her.

A FINAL PLEA

On 27 April Anne addresses a final plea to Thomas Cromwell.

Prays for a lease of Loddyngton, co. Leicester, lately granted to Crumwell. Prays to be released from her husband's debts.

Calendar of State Papers Relating to Ireland, 1509–1573, Longman, Green, Longman and Roberts, London (1860)

Ursula, Lady St Leger

Ursula St Leger was the wife of Sir Warham St Leger, grandson of Sir Anthony St Leger, a former Lord Deputy, who died in 1559. There was a revolt in Munster, led by James Fitzmaurice FitzGerald, cousin of the Earl of Desmond.

A Prayer for her Security

In this letter, dated 18 June 1569, from Cork, to the Lord Deputy, Lady St Leger briefly describes the course of the revolt so far. Her concern for her own safety was well founded, for the rebels had vowed 'never to depart from Cork, unless the Mayor deliver out of the town the Lady Sentleger'.

Lady Ursula Sentleger to [the same]. On Wednesday the Sheriff went for England. Next morning James Fitzmaurice with 4,000 spoiled Kerrycurrihy; on Friday they took Tracton and killed John Enchedon and all her men; on Saturday they came to the castle of Carigyleyn. The enemies were informed by the tenants what victual and provision was in the castle. Prays that some order may be taken for her security.

ed. H.C. Hamilton, *Calendar of State Papers – Ireland, Elizabeth*,
Eyre and Spottiswood, London (1890)

Lady Fytzwylliam

The very day her husband, Lord Justice Fytzwylliam, was made Lord Deputy of Ireland, she felt it necessary to make provision for the future.

Provision for the Future

Possibly because she was well aware of how easily good and lengthy service to the crown could be disregarded, she wrote to Queen Elizabeth on 11 December 1571.

Petition of Lady Fytzwylliam to the Queen, to have such consideration of her husband, now Lord Deputy of Ireland, that if God should call him in this service his posterity should not be undone by the great debt that he oweth to Her Majesty, by reason of his long service in that realm.

ed. H.C. Hamilton, *Calendar of State Papers – Ireland, Elizabeth*,
Eyre and Spottiswood, London (1890)

Katherin Eggarton

Katherin was the wife of one Captain Eggarton, who had more or less abandoned her and their children in Ireland, while he took himself off to London, to seek his fortune, it would appear.

A WIFE'S PLEA TO HER HUSBAND

After a period of living in, at least, reduced circumstances, poor Katherin writes to her husband at Court in London, in this letter sent from Carrickfergus on 11 November 1589. Her husband, who is in fact sick, appeals to Lord Burghley through his secretary, on 22 December. Unfortunately we do not know whether the appeal was successful, or, indeed, what Katherin's fate was.

My good Charles,

I have received from you since your arrival in England one letter, wherein you use your wonted fair and gentle persuasions for me to hold myself patiently contented, and that your great hope is you shall be speedily despatched, but how soon soever I greatly fear the same will come too late for my relief; for what with thy absence, the remembrance of my sweet father's death, your unwise dealings in selling mine annuity, my chain (chenne), and my bordars, only for the relief of a company of most ungrateful men who do daily exclaim of you, and threaten me to take my clothes to pawn for victuals; adding hereunto my miserable fare, sometimes glad to drink water with no other bread than that which is made of this country barley. All these occasions weighed, you may very easily persuade yourself I suffer no small extremities of grief. Your three children be in good health, whom I wish with myself in heaven, where for my own part I trust, through my sweet Saviour Jesus Christ, to be before you shall see my face again, humbly praying thee to bring my children up in the fear of God, and give them learning, so far forth as thy ability will extend unto. And so she, the most unfortunate in this world of all her kindred, as a most obedient wife taketh her leave.

ed. H.C. Hamilton, *Calendar of State Papers Relating to Ireland, Elizabeth*, Eyre and Spottiswood, London (1890)

Joan Moclere

Joan was, as she says, daughter and heir to Richard Moclere, who had been the owner of various lands in County Tipperary. Unfortunately, while she was under the age of seven, her patrimony was wrongfully taken from her.

A WRONGED WOMAN SEEKS JUSTICE

After a strange delay of twenty-four years Joan seeks justice from the Lord Deputy FitzWilliam, in this petition of 14 February 1590. Fortunately for Joan she received it, at least to some degree. Her case was referred to Mr Justice Gold and Mr Thomas Wadding who ordered that she be paid for her interest in the property and that she should have the rents and issue thereof until she be wholly paid and satisfied.

She states that she is the daughter and lawful heir to Richard Moclere of Ballicereghane in the county of the Cross of Tipperary, deceased, who died seized of certain lands in Ballicereghane, viz., Garryvicnicolays, Stangrioghe, Leakavony, Gorticnock, Gwertinediner, Dyoth Lyasrioghe, Gertyparck and eight other gardens, the Priest's garden with four acres and a half of the large measure of the country, &c., which lands and tenements descended unto her as lawful heir unto, her father, until about 24 years past when she being under seven years of age, Patrick Sherlock of Waterford, gentleman, late deceased, wrongfully entered into the premises and converted the same to his own use without any colour of right, as also John Sherlock, son and heir to the said Patrick, of his mere wrong and with strength (force) did withold during his lifetime to her destruction. All which time your poor complainant during these three years past has been a suiter unto the late Lord Deputy Sir John Perrot, who referred the matter to the Lord of Cahir with the referment of Sir Thomas Norreys, the Vice-President of Munster, to take order therein, who accordingly standing upon the examination of certain gentlemen, freeholders and husbandmen of the country there, did find your complainant to be lawful heir of the premises, and thereupon did draw out an order for your complainant to have the possession of the said lands, which order being drawn, yet would not he perfect the same until he had seen what title or good matter the executors of the said John Sherlock could bring against your complainant's right in the said lands. And for the better doing thereof gave the said executors three months space for the same, and yet could not find any good matter against your complainant's right in the said lands, but what by sinister practices and false detractions and drawing (*sic*) of time to fatigue your suppliant being poor and unable to follow her matter, which the said Lord of Cahir perceiving, and your complainant to have right interest did put her in possession as well by the referment of the said vice-president as also the justices there in that province of Munster. And the same did possess and enjoy all this 12 months past until now of late Ellice Butler, wife to the said John Sherlocke, one of the executors, did wrongfully cause your poor complainant to be dispossessed to her undoing. And for that she is not able to prosecute her cause by due course of law unless your honour will take order therein in admitting her in forma pauperis, which is her desire.

ed. H.C. Hamilton, *Calendar of State Papers Relating to Ireland, Elizabeth*, Eyre and Spottiswood, London (1890)

Mary Carleill

A part from the fact that she was married, and a loyal, defensive wife, nothing more is known of Mary Carleill.

GOVERNMENTS WERE ALWAYS THE SLOWEST PAYERS

In this letter of 10 July 1592, to Burghley, Mary adroitly urges the repayment of monies owed to her husband by the government. We can only hope that her appeal was successful!

May it please you to understand that there is due to my husband, Mr Carleill, and to his small company, the sum of 1,000*l.* or thereabouts, as, by warrants, signed by the Lord Deputy and Council in Ireland, which are now in Sir Henry Wallop's hands, doth appear. I know my husband has acquainted you with our need, which, I assure you, is rather more than otherwise, and therefore to rehearse the same now would be but troublesome to you, and but grief to myself. Now understanding that there is a Privy Seal for Ireland, I am most humbly to beseech you to vouchsafe your favour so far as to be means that some half or third part of the said arrearage may be paid. And as my husband has been ever bound to you, so shall we never cease to pray for your happiness and prosperity.

ed. H.C. Hamilton, *Calendar of State Papers Relating to Ireland, Elizabeth*, Longman, London (1885)

Gráinne ní Mhaille

Gráinne ní Mhaille is better – though slightly incorrectly – known as 'Grace O'Malley', since the Irish name 'Gráinne' has no connection with 'Grace'. First married to Donall O'Flaherty and then to Sir Richard Burke, Gráinne had enjoyed considerable notoriety through much of the later sixteenth century as a sort of female pirate in the West of Ireland, successfully beating off an attacking force from Galway in 1574. In 1583, after the death of her second husband, she is said to have retired to her fortress at Carrigahowley, Co. Mayo, 'with all her followers and 1,000 head of cattle and mares'. In July 1593 she was required to respond to eighteen 'articles of interrogatory'.

GRÁINNE'S ANSWERS TO THE ARTICLES OF INTERROGATORY

The eighteen articles of interrogatory to which Gráinne was required to respond covered her parentage, her marriages, her issue, her territory and her financial status. Her letter is full and revealing.

To the first. – Her father was called Doodarro O'Mailly, sometime chieftain of the country called Opper Owle O'Mailly, now called the Barony of Murasky [Murrisk]; her mother was called Margaret ny Mailly, daughter to Conogher O'Mailly of the same country and family. The whole country of Owle O'Mailly aforesaid have these islands, viz, Inish Boffyny, Clerie, Inish Twirke, Inisharke, Caher, Inishdalluff, Devellan, and other small islands of little value, which and the rest of the mainland, are divided into towns to the number of twenty; and to every town four quarters, or ploughs of land, is assigned; out of every such quarter of land is yearly paid to Her Majesty ten shillings, called the composition rent. There is also in Connaught a country called Owle Eighter, otherwise the Lower or Nether Owle, containing fifty towns, at four quarters the town, yearly paying the same rent, whereof the Sept of the Mailles in general hath twenty towns, the Bourkes of MacWilliam's country other twenty towns, and the Earl of Ormond ten towns.

To the second. – Her first husband was called Donell Ichoggy O'Flaherty, and during his life chieftain of the Barony of Ballynehenessy, containing twenty-four towns at four quarters of land to every town, paying yearly the composition rent aforesaid. After his death Teige O'Flaherty, the eldest son of Sir Morough [Ne Doe O'Flaherty], now at court, entered into Bally-ne-heussy aforesaid, there did build a strong castle, and the same with the demesne lands thereof kept many years, which Teige in the last rebellion of his father was slain.

To the third. – She had two sons by her said first husband, the eldest, called Owen O'Flaherty, married Katherine Bourke, daughter to Edmond Bourke, of Castle Barry; by her he had a son named Donnell O'Flaherty, now living, which Owen all his lifetime remained a true subject to Her Majesty under the government of Sir Nicholas Malby while he lived, and under Sir Richard Bingham until July 1586, at which time the Bourkes of McWilliam's country and the Sept of the Shoose began to rebel. The said Owen, according to Sir Richard's special direction, did withdraw himself, his followers, and tenants, with all their goods and cattle, into a strong island, for their more and better assurance. There have been sent against the said rebels 500 soldiers under the leading of Captain John Bingham, appointed by his brother Sir Richard Bingham as his lieutenant in those parts, when they missed both the rebels and their cattle, they came to the mainland right against the said island calling for victuals; whereupon the said Owen came forth with a number of boats and ferried all the soldiers into the island, where they were entertained with the best cheer they had. That night the said Owen was apprehended and tied with a rope with 18 of his chief followers; in the morning the soldiers drew out of the island four thousand cows, five hundred stud mares and horses, and a thousand sheep, leaving the remainder of the poor men all naked within the island; [they] came with the cattle and prisoners to Bally-ne-heussy aforesaid, where John Bingham aforesaid stayed for their coming; that evening he caused the said 18 persons, without trial or good cause, to be hanged, among whom was hanged a gentleman of land and living, called Thebault O'Tool, being of the age of four score and ten years. The next night following a false alarm was raised in the camp in the dead of the night, the said Owen being fast bound in the cabin of Captain Grene O'Molloy, and at that instant the said Owen was cruelly murdered, having 12 deadly wounds, and in that miserable sort he ended his years and unfortunate days. Captain William Mostyn now at court, Captain Meriman and Captain Mordant were of that company. Her second son, called Morrough O'Flaherty, now living, is married to Honora Bourke, daughter to Richard Bourke of Deriviclaghny, in the Magheri Reogh within the county of Galway.

To the fourth. – Morrough her second son of aforesaid and Donnell son to her first son the aforesaid Owen murdered, do possess and enjoy the fourth part of the Barony of Ballyneheussy aforesaid unto them descended from their ancestors, which is all the maintenance they have.

To the fifth. – This is answered more at large in the answer to the third article.

To the sixth. – Her first husband by the mother's side of Sir Morrough [O'Flaherty] now at court was his cousin german, and also cousins, both being descended of one stock and root, of nine degrees of consanguinity asunder.

To the seventh. – Her second husband was called Sir Richard Bourke, knight, *alias* McWilliam, chief of the Bourkes of Nether or Low

Connaught, by him she hath a son called Theobald Bourke now living, he is married to Mewffe O'Connor sister to O'Connor Sligo now at Court, his inheritance is about 40 quarters of land situated in the three Baronies of Carry [Carra], Nether Owle, and Galling [Gallen].

To the eighth. – The countries of Connaught among the Irishry never yielded any thirds to any woman surviving the chieftain whose rent was uncertain, for the most part extorted, but now made certain by the composition, and all Irish exactions merely abolished.

To the ninth. – The composition provided nothing to relieve the wife of any chieftain after his death, wherein no mention is made of any such.

To the 10th. – Among the Irishry the custom is, that wives shall have but her first dowry without any increase or allowance for the same, time out of mind it hath been so used, and before any woman do deliver up her marriage to her husband she receives sureties for the restitution of the same in manner and form as she hath delivered it, in regard that husbands through their great expenses, especially chieftains at the time of their deaths, have no goods to leave behind them, but are commonly indebted, at other times they are devorced upon proof of precontracts; and the husband now and then without any lawful or due proceeding 'do put his wife from him' and so bringeth in another; so as the wife is to have sureties for her dowery for fear of the worse.

To the 11th. – After the death of her last husband she gathered together all her own followers and with 1,000 head of cows and mares departed and became a dweller in Carrikkhowlly in Borosowle, parcel of the Earl of Ormond's lands in Connaught, and in the year 1586, after the murdering of her son Owen, the rebellion being then in Connaught, Sir Richard Bingham granted her his letters of 'twision' [tuition] against all men and willed her to remove from her late dwelling at Borosowle and to come and dwell under him, in her journey as she travelled, was encountered by the five bands of soldiers, under the leading of John Bingham, and thereupon she was apprehended and tied in a rope, both she and her followers at that instant were spoiled of their said cattle and of all that ever they had besides the same, and brought to Sir Richard who caused a new pair of gallows to be made for her last funeral where she thought to end her days, she was let at liberty upon the hostage and pledge of one Richard Bourke otherwise called the Devil's Hook. When he did rebel fear compelled her to fly by sea into Ulster, and there with O'Neill and O'Donnell staid three months; her galleys by a tempest being broken. She returned to Connaught and in Dublin received Her Majesty's gracious pardon by Sir John Perrot six years past and was so made free. Ever since she dwelleth in Connaught a farmer's life, very poor, bearing cess; and paying Her Majesty's composition rent, utterly did give over her former trade of maintenance by sea and land.

To the 12th. – Walter Bourke, FitzThebault, and Shane Bourke FitzMeiller are cousins german removed of one side, viz, Walter, son to Thebauth, son to Walter Faddy Bourke *alias* Long Walter Bourke, Shane, aforesaid son to Meiller, son to the said Walter Faddy Thebault Bourke mentioned in the seventh article, and born by Grany Ny Mailly son to Sir Richard Bourke, her last husband, which Sir Richard was brother to the said Walter Faddy.

To the 13th. – The country of her first husband is situated between Owle O'Mailly on the north west part, MacWilliam's country on the north east towards the county of Sligo, Sir Morrough O'Flaherty's country, on the east side towards Galway and the great Bay of Galway on the south.

To the 14th. – The castle, town, and lands of Morisky is possessed by Owen M'Thomas O'Mailly now chieftain by the name of O'Mailly.

To the 15th. – The MacGibbons have no lands by inheritance in any part of the country; farmers they are at will both to the Bourkes and to the O'Maillies.

To the 16th. – She doth not know or understand Caremore or Moinconnell.

To the 17th. – The island of Ackill is occupied by some of the Maillys as tenants to the Earl of Ormond, as for Kill Castle, she knoweth no town of that name.

To the 18th. – Her last husband had two brothers Walter and Ullugge [Ulick] Bourke, both died before she married Sir Richard Bourke her said husband, their father was called David Bourke.

A PETITION TO THE QUEEN

Shortly after her response to the articles of interrogatory Gráinne ní
Mhaille petitions Queen Elizabeth.

For maintenance. Prays that her two sons and their cousins Walter
Burghke Fitz Theobald Reogh, and Shane Burghk MacMoiler may have
their lands by patent on surrender.

THE TIGRESS APPEALS FOR SUPPORT

In the hope of influencing Queen Elizabeth Gráinne appeals to Burghley
for support – and adds a rider to show that she remains a tigress after all.

To be a mean to Her Majesty to grant her some reasonable maintenance.
The Lord Deputy to accept the surrender of her sons, the heirs of
O'Flaherty, and M'William Bourk. Grany Ne Mally desires Her Majesty's
letter under her hand for license during her life to invade with sword and
fire all Her Majesty's enemies.

ed. H.C. Hamilton, *Calendar of State Papers Relating to Ireland,*
Elizabeth, Eyre and Spottiswood, London (1890)

THE
SEVENTEENTH
CENTURY

The seventeenth century was a period of confusion, with changes not only of monarchs but even more confusing changes during the Protectorate. Against this striking political background there continued to be regular appearances of impoverished widows like Mary Preston and Mary, Baroness Widdrington. More interestingly, there appear women, like Susanna O'Brien and Lady Belhaven, who were prepared to undertake on their husbands' behalf requests, even demands, for justice. There are, too, embarrassing and even bewildering confusions about religion, as shown by Lady Falkland's unfortunate case. Happily, as a kind of counter-balance, there are items like the simple, honest and totally appealing letter of thanks from Dorothy, Lady Rawdon, to her brother, with the promise of an equally appealing token of gratitude.

Almost as comic relief there is the strange petition by Katherine Fitzgerald to the Archbishop of Canterbury. Even for the seventeenth century, the notion of a marriage between a seven-year-old boy and a girl of thirteen is disconcerting.

Lady Stewart O'Donnell

The O'Donnells were a very important Irish family. It is not quite clear how Lady Stewart (or Stuart, as she is described in another letter) was connected.

A POOR PENSIONER

In this letter of 24 September 1625, Lady Stewart writes to Lord Conway asking for help.

Asking that Lord Conway will move the Lord Deputy to make her payment of 50l. a year passed to her by her father-in-law, Mr. Barnwell. Her present pension from the King is very small.

STILL A POOR PENSIONER

In March 1626, Lady Stewart was obliged to write again to Lord Conway asking for help.

Excuses her sudden departure from England owing to the smallness of her means and the fear of losing her reputation. She is anxious to draw her brother into the King's service. This she could do were he not smarting under great losses and a sense of his own innocence. She awaits an intimation of His Majesty's intention towards herself and her brother.

ed. R.P. Mahaffy, *Calendar of State Papers – Ireland, Charles I,* Eyre & Spottiswood, London (1900)

Lady Falkland

Lady Falkland was the wife of Henry Cary, who, as Lord Falkland, had been appointed Lord Deputy in 1622. In 1624 he had received permission to publish a proclamation against priests and instructions to enforce the laws against recusants; a year later he was forbidden to enforce that proclamation.

AN EMBARRASSING CONFESSION

In this undated letter, received by her husband on Christmas Day 1626, Lady Falkland confesses to her husband that she is, after all, a papist, and has been consorting with priests. He is of the opinion that the only way to reclaim his apostate wife is to send her to her mother. In April 1627 he records that he is angry with her for not going to her mother, having obtained the delay through 'feminine wily pretences', and vows to obtain a complete divorce if she does not comply with his wishes.

You charge me with fostering priests and Jesuits. I have never seen a Jesuit but have conversed with priests. One man may have supped with me, but I never provided specially for them, and since it pleased His Majesty to make me, whether 'I would or no, declare myself Catholic', which is on Tuesday last a month, there is not, &c.

ed. R.P. Mahaffy, *Calendar of State Papers – Ireland, Charles I,* Eyre & Spottiswood, London (1900)

Mary Preston

Mary Preston was the widow of Colonel Francis Netterville, and found herself totally destitute.

A PETITION TO THE KING

Like so many others before – and after – her, Mary finds it necessary, in 1660, to petition King Charles II in the hope that she may obtain compensation for her losses.

Colonel Francis Nettervile's father had but an estate tail 'in the lands which he was seized' and if his said father acted anything contrary to loyalty, his said son could not suffer for it. The Duke of Ormond, when Lord Lieutenant of Ireland, restored Col. Nettervile to his estate on account of his merit and services. He was accordingly seized of a good estate in the county and city of Dublin and (in consideration of a marriage had and solemnised between him and the petitioner, who is the daughter of Viscount Taragh, deceased, and of a great sum paid by Lord Taragh over and above the jointure settled on her at her marriage) by his last will bequeathed all his estate to the petitioner. Besides land in the co. Dublin and houses in the city of Dublin, this estate consisted of interest in a mortgage of 1,000*l.* which he had in the co. Longford, as may appear by his last will, &c.

Col. Francis Nettervile, finding the power of the late usurped Government in Ireland to be prevalent, 'did, rather than live under their tyranny, withdraw himself and family into Spain, and having the command of some forces in Catalonia he there departed this life, leaving the petitioner an afflicted widow in foreign parts.' His whole estate had been seized by the usurpers on account of his loyalty. The petitioner has supported this in hopes of the King's restoration, which is now come to pass.

She prays for restoration to the estate of her deceased husband, as aforesaid settled and disposed of, for her livelihood.

ed R.B. Mahaffy, *Calendar of State Papers – Ireland, Charles II*, Wyman & Co., London (1910)

Margaret Blake

Margaret Blake was a widow, and her husband a member of one of the fourteen 'tribes' of Galway. The Blakes, like other prominent Galway families, had been primarily traders. Their special trading interests lay in the West Indies.

A PETITION TO THE KING

In this petition of 1660 to Charles II, Margaret Blake seeks redress for injustices suffered by her family and for restitution, not only for herself and her daughter, also called Margaret, but also her son-in-law, Matthew Quinn.

The petitioners and their predecessors maintained the town of Galway for your Majesty's use in the late wars 'above 16 years' and disbursed 60,000*l.* therein, and lent the Duke of Ormond and Marquis of Clanrickard 30,000*l.* more. They never submitted to the King's enemies till your Majesty commanded them to yield and make their quarters by your own letter dated at Paris in 1651. At Paris and Brussells your Majesty promised the petitioner Quin that you would remember him in England for his loyalty. This can be proved by certificates from the Dukes of Gloucester and Ormond, the Earl of Calinforth [Carlingford] and Lord Taffe.

The petitioners' estate in Ireland is given away from them and they are left in an almost starving condition.

They pray that their condition may be considered and a grant made to them of twelve of their houses there [in Galway], which your Majesty has bestowed on Sir Thomas Clarges; also that your Majesty will prevail with the Duke of York to give up to them his interest in 10,000 acres of land in the co. Galway, which formerly belonged for the most part to their relations.

IF AT FIRST . . .

Whether her petition of 1660 was completely successful or not, she found it necessary to submit a second petition in 1662.

Petitioners have been constantly loyal to the King and 'ran' with your Majesty's fortunes abroad during the Usurper's government, during which time they have been relieved and maintained by the King in Spain. The petitioner Quin served your Majesty at that time loyally, as may appear by several certificates, and the King, at Paris and Brussels, granted him the perquisites and profits of the collection of quit rent in the cos. Galway and Mayo, but the enjoyment of this has been kept from him. Quin ventured whatever he had or could procure from his friends in a cargo of goods and merchandizes and 'being in his course at sea in the late Dutch wars' was taken, and lost all.

By this he and the other petitioners, who depend on him, being forgotten in the Acts of Settlement, are in great want and even in a starving condition.

They pray for 1,000*l*. out of the Customs, ingate and outgate, of Galway on goods exported or imported by themselves or by such of their relations as they shall give a list of to the officers of the port, whereby the Customs will be advanced there, the merchants now idle encouraged to trade and the petitioners come to a good way of subsistence.

ed. R.B. Mahaffy, *Calendar of State Papers – Ireland, Charles II,*
Wyman & Co., London (1910)

Dorothy, Lady Rawdon

Lady Rawdon was the sister of Edward, Viscount Conway and Killulta. He died in 1683, but had clearly shown great care and kindness to his sister and her family.

A VERY PERSONAL LETTER

In this letter of 31 August 1669, Lady Rawdon expresses her gratitude, in very simple terms, for kindnesses shown to her family. 'Usquebath' is an English version of the Irish word for whiskey.

I thank you for your constant goodness to Arthur and grieve to hear my mother is so ill of ague. Mr Mease [Mace] is, I fear, dying. He was insensible yesterday, but is sensible to-day. He will be a great loss, and his wife and children will be left in a sad condition. 'I have provided twelve barrells of scollops for your Lordship and some usquebath, which I intend to send to Bromeiam [Birmingham].' I will send word when they are despatched.

> Your most sincere affectionate sister and humble servant,
>
> Do. Rawdon.

> ed. R.B. Mahaffy, *Calendar of State Papers – Ireland, Charles II*, Wyman & Co., London (1910)

Mary, Baroness Widdrington

L ady Widdrington was the widow of William, Lord Widdrington, who was killed in the king's service.

AN IMPOVERISHED WIDOW

In 1670 Mary, finding herself 'reduced to poverty', petitions King Charles II in the hope that at long last she may obtain some relief.

Petitioner's husband, William, Lord Widdrington, was killed in your Majesty's service without having made any provision for payment of the great debts he had contracted – in prosecuting the war for King Charles I and your Majesty, – or for preferment of his younger children. Petitioner was consequently reduced to poverty and asked your Majesty for the fines of Munster, Leinster, Connaught and Clare for a livelihood. Your Majesty on August 2, recommended the petition to the Lord Deputy, for which she returns thanks. On applying to the Lord Deputy, she learned that the grant of these fines would be a lessening of your Majesty's revenue in Ireland and of uncertain profit to her.

Your Majesty wrote to the petitioner's husband that if any disaster befel him in the business of Worcester you would care for the petitioner.

She has long waited your Majesty's pleasure therein, and now asks for a 'yearly livelihood' of 300*l.* to be charged on the Customs of Wexford in Ireland towards her maintenance and the payment of the great debts owing to her. She is informed by the Earl of Bristow [Bristol] that your Majesty gave her last petition specially in charge to Sir Edward Nicholas. Her case is different from others, owing to her great sufferings.

ed. R.B. Mahaffy, *Calendar of State Papers – Ireland, Charles II*,
Wyman & Co., London (1910)

Susanna O'Brien

As she says, Susanna O'Brien was the wife of Colonel Murtagh O'Brien; whether she was more literate than her husband or simply had more determination is not clear.

ANOTHER PETITIONING WIFE

Once again, it is the woman who is determined to petition King Charles II to request a reward for loyalty and service.

Her husband Col. Mortagh O'Bryen for his constant loyalty (he was one of the last to hold out for the King in Ireland) was banished. He then went with 1,500 men to Flanders, resolved rather to die than to serve under the Usurper. He continued under your Majesty's ensigns until the Restoration, and then transported himself hither in order to serve further. Her father was mortally wounded under the Duke of York at Dunkirk, and your petitioner's marriage portion of 3,000*l.* was wholly spent in preserving the model of your Majesty's forces together in Ireland till the time of their transportation.

She prays for the right to create a Viscount in Ireland.

ed. R.B. Mahaffy, Calendar of State Papers – Ireland, Charles II,
Wyman & Co., London (1910)

Lady Belhaven

Unfortunately neither Lady Belhaven nor her husband secured a major place in Irish history; it would appear, however, that she was the more energetic of the two.

GIVE ME LAND . . .

In or about May 1661, Lady Belhaven found it necessary to petition Charles II to obtain for herself and her husband land in Ireland to sustain them.

By your Majesty's reference the Attorney General was directed to consider the validity of a patent granted to the petitioner's husband of the Mews Keeper's place and other houses in the name of Andrew Cole your Majesty's equerry, who hath not surrendered it in favour of any, to the petitioner's prejudice.

The Attorney General, on perusal, has declared this patent good.

Notwithstanding the said legal right and your Majesty's gracious commands that the petitioner shall have quiet possession of the place, 'the Lord General, Master of the Horse, doth so eagerly pursue the extorting the said place that your petitioner can expect no peace in the enjoyment thereof if not by frequent and unpardonable troubling your sacred Majesty.' Rather than do this the petitioner will surrender the post to be disposed of by your Majesty.

The King granted to the petitioner in 1641 th[ree] thousand acres in Ireland, but, by reason of the rebellion there and the death of the Earl of Strafford, the plantation failed. In consequence the petitioner failed to get any benefit by her grant.

She asks for a grant of the bog of Allen in the co. Kildare, containing 3,000 acres. This was formerly in the possession of Philip Fitzgerald, Esq., and is now in your Majesty's hands by reason of his rebellion in 1641, and 'also of his betraying your Majesty's forces under the conduct of the Marquis of —— proved in Ireland and several other treasons' as is by himself proved and recorded in the Court at Arklow, thereby to 'ingratiate with Oliver Cromwell,' who conferred many courtesies on him, giving him much land in the province of Ulster, where he is now planted.

A YEAR LATER . . .

Having failed to obtain the 3,000 acres in the Bog of Allen, in 1661 Lady Belhaven found it necessary once again to petition the King.

Your Majesty asked the petitioner to surrender her patent under the Great Seal of the Keeper's place in the Mews and of her house therein; and your petitioner obeyed. Your Majesty then granted her Philip Fitzgerald's land in the co. Kildare in Ireland, passing your Royal word the same should be your petitioner's whenas it should be made appear that your Majesty was entitled to that land or, otherwise, the equivalent of that land. If your Majesty's promise could be transmitted to posterity the petitioner is sure that she would not need to supplicate for any other evidence.

As your Majesty has thought fit, by your Declaration for the settlement of Ireland, to dispose of these lands otherwise, the petitioner, asks for 3,000 acres of land in the co. Dublin. These will give her and her husband a support after long services.

ed. R.B. Mahaffy, Calendar of State Papers – Ireland, Charles II,
Wyman & Co., London (1910)

Martha Hatt

Martha Hatt is described as 'alias Arundel', possibly her maiden name. She terms herself 'an oppressed and aged widow'.

'PRINCELY DEBONARITY'

This charming phrase is used by Martha in her petition of November 1662 to the king and privy council in her attempt to relieve her oppressed state.

She is an oppressed and aged widow and shews on behalf of herself and her family that: –

She petitioned the King in Council on the second of this month, and thereupon had an order of reference to the Earl of Orrery and the rest of the Commissioners from Ireland to take consideration thereof and to prepare a provisional clause for her relief in the Declaration for Ireland, or otherwise to certify to your Majesty the grounds why such a provision ought not to be inserted.

There is not any provisional clause prepared for her relief, but the said Commissioners say she is already provided for in the Declaration with others in the like condition. What provisions these are she does not know, but she does know that 'if your Majesty of your princely debonarity' does not order her to be paid, (with the adventurers for lands in Ireland and the officers of this present army) for her husband's service as cornet to the troop of horse under Robert, Lord Dillon both before and during the rebellion, and for her husband's horses, arms, provisions, and ready moneys lent by her in 1643 and 1644, she and hers may perish by pining want. She has suffered for 20 years, her husband having been killed in service against the Irish rebels in 1643, having done very good service against them and having lost a very good estate, as appears by several authentic certificates in the hands of Sir Richard Fanshawe and Sir George Lane.

When she might have recovered her ruined estate after judgment decree and execution was obtained by her at great expense, she lost all by illegal protections given by Sir Theophilus Jones.

Notwithstanding she had an order in 1657 from the then power from this Board commanding that her said decree should be satisfied in Ireland and that the then Lord Deputy and Council should take care for her relief: yet to this day she has never received any manner of relief and 'her husband's blood postponed' and all her other debts, merely because he served, and her debt accrued, before the 5th day of June, 1649.

There is no case like the petitioner's in the whole of Ireland. Her husband served long and loyally: he and she were Protestants and natives of England and she was outed of her whole estate by the rebellion; 'yet by the power, malice, and potency of Miles Corbet, the then Lord Chief Baron, Sir Hardress Waller, Major Antony Morgan and the aforesaid Sir Theophilus Jones is she deprived of the benefit of the just laws of the land.'

She prays for full satisfaction for her husband's faithful service done in Ireland for the Crown of England. Other widows whose husbands served in Ireland even since 5 June, 1649, have long had that satisfaction in the co. Dublin. She asks for payment for all horses, arms, provisions and money provided by her in 1643 and 1644 and that she may have the benefit of her just proceedings and decree according to former orders from this Board in 1657 with such additional costs and charges as your Majesty may think meet. She also asks for an allowance to pay her debts here and transport her and her distressed family into Ireland.

AN ADDITIONAL MEMORIAL

To support her petition Martha attaches an additional memorial.

Repeats the substance of the foregoing.

Begins 'Remember now upon the settling of the Irish lands on the adventurers for land in Ireland the unparallelled case of the widow of Cornet Simon Hatt,' &c. *Gives* the following reasons in her favour.

1. Her husband was a member of the old standing army of Ireland and was commanded to his garrison at midnight, leaving your petitioner and his family to the cruelty of the merciless enemy. He saw his family and home no more.

2. Her husband had a considerable sum of money due to him when the rebellion began, as appears from Lord Robert Dillon's muster-rolls.

3. Officers who served in Ireland since 5 June, 1649, have got estates in Ireland, but she, whose husband served before that, has lost one.

4. The Parliamentary power appointed that the widows and orphans of officers and soldiers who had done faithful service against the Irish rebels should be provided for. Petitioner has had nothing but promises.

6. [*sic*]. She thinks none were greater adventurers in Ireland than those who adventured both and life and estate, and asks for a provisional clause in the Declaration for Ireland. She has suffered for upwards of 20 years. Prays for mercy.

ed. R.B. Mahaffy, Calendar of State Papers – Ireland – Charles II,
Wyman & Co., London (1910)

Katherine Fitzgerald

Katherine was a daughter of John and Katherine Fitzgerald and became the ward of her uncle, Lord Power of Curraghmore, Earl of Tyrone, on the death of her father in 1664. In 1673, however, her uncle – for reasons not totally unconnected with his own greed – had arranged a marriage between Katherine, who was then but thirteen years of age, and his own eldest son, John Power, who was then only seven.

A PETITION

This is Katherine's petition, in the form of a letter, to the Archbishop of Canterbury, protesting at her rather bizarre marriage.

In the name of God. Amen. Whereas I Katherine FitzGerald, sole daughter and heiress of John FitzGerald, late of Decies and County of Waterford within the kingdom of Ireland, deceased, did on or about the 20th of May Anno Domini 1673 without due consideration, or the consent of my guardians – intrusted by my late father, solemnize or contract marriage or esposals, or rather the show and form thereof, with the Right Honourable John now Lord

Decies, then the Hon. John Power alias le Power Esquire, an infant of the age of seven years, which said contract was performed and celebrated the day and year above said, before his Grace the Most Reverend Father in God, Gilbert Lord Archbishop of Canterbury, Primate of all England and Metropolitan and divers other witnesses, being now at my own perfect liberty and having freedome to express my voluntary and spontaneous inclination as to the same and to set forth the means whereby I was there unto induced.

I do by these presents before your Grace, the notary publique and other witnesses hereunto subscribed, protest, aver and declare for the truth, that the said contract or rather show and form there off, was unduly and contrary to my own pure will and good liking obtained from me, and that I had not expressed or given any colour of consent there unto, by imoderate importunity threats, fear and the false suggestions of loosing the estate in Ireland descended unto me by the death of my late father, and for as much as I have bin hitherto restrained and hindered from manifestation of my dislike and dissent to the said pretended contract (which if I had enjoyed my perfect liberty I should otherwise have done) I doe by these presents totally and absolutely disclaim, renounce and recede from the same and every part thereoff, and we declare that there lyes no obligation upon me for either the perfection or consumation of the said pretended espousals or contract of marriage with the said Rt Hon. John Lord Decies, for or by reason of any consent by me pretended to be interposed in manner as afore said, but 'that the same was, and is in itself' null and void, and to all intents and purposes either in relation to my person or estate) is and ought to be esteemed and adjudged as an act utterly invalid and ineffectual, and I doe desire the witnesses here present to beare testimony hereof and the same may be intended amongst the records and muniments of your Graces principal Registry and letters testimonial hereof and the same may be entered, made and delivered unto me for the better creditt and confirmation of the truth of all and singular the premisses.

Given under my hand and seal this tenth day of May in the year
of our Lord 1675 signed
Katherine FitzGerald

DISSIMULATION

In this letter to her uncle, Richard Francklin, Katherine speaks as if her marriage was null and void, but her reference to the Earl of Londonderry as having become 'her humble servant' and dutifully asking her uncle's opinion as to his suitability as a husband does rather savour of dissimulation, for in 1676 she effected a runaway marriage with Edward Villiers, eldest son of George, 4th Viscount Grandison.

21 SEPTEMBER, 1675

Dear Uncle,

Y^{rs} of the seaventh of this month came to my hands a saturday last with ye long expected newes of yor safe arrival at Youghall and yor good successe with my servants, both wch reijoiced me extreamily. As to that of Mr Theophillus Jones, my Lord of Ossory hath acquainted the King with itt, whereupon Mr. Mulys appointed to draw a letter to be sent from his Matie to Theophillus for the stopping of any proceeding to be made by him therein. My Lord of Ossory did likewise desire his Matie that a patent should be granted unto me of my estate, whereunto the King answered that it should be done whenever I pleased, according to my former promise that I would not marry anyone without first acquainting you of itt. I thought fitt to lett you know that the Earle of Londonderry is become my humble servant whose estate (is said to be worth £4,500 per ann) Wherefore Lister desires me to enquire of his Estate, and in your next to give your advice therin. I pray lett the £200 which I wrote for, be sent as soon as you can for I am sure you cannot be ignorant of my present want thereof. And as to the reference wh^{ch} you wrote of there is no such thing, neither was it in the least mentioned to me or my Lord of Ossory but Tyrone is just as he was when you were here. And pray remember my duty to my grandmother, my service to my Aunt and love to my couzens, which is all at present from

Yo^{re} affectionate niece and servant,

Katherine FitzGerald.

Thérese Muir McKenzie, *Dromana: The Memoirs of an Irish Family*, Sealy, Bryers and Walker, Dublin (n.d.)

THE
EIGHTEENTH
CENTURY

The eighteenth century comes as a refreshing novelty, with a relatively sudden flowering of letters written purely for social reasons, as a means of conveying to friends and relations some insight into people's views and aspirations. While complaints about penury and corruption and petitions for justice certainly continued, they are no longer as dominant a force in the annals of women's letters. As a welcome relief we have rather frivolous letters from Mary Delany to her sister, describing the high life in Dublin and the delights of the Irish countryside.

To a certain extent as a contrast, we also have the more serious contribution of the McCracken family, caught up in the rather curious post-French Revolution political scene in the North of Ireland. The mother, Ann, cares for and worries about her daughter, Mary Ann, writing to her in Dublin, where she was attending on her brother, Henry Joy McCracken, imprisoned there for his involvement with the United Irishmen. Mary Ann herself makes a very strong appearance: her care for her brother (Harry) dominates her life until his public execution in Belfast, and is followed by her love for one of her brother's fellow revolutionaries, Thomas Russell. Her care was not, however, focused solely on her family: throughout her life she showed great consideration towards not only her own workers, but to workers in general, as her letter to the Belfast Newsletter *– the paper founded in 1737 by her grandfather, Francis Joy – clearly indicates. The Joys and the McCrackens exemplify the better type of Ulster entrepreneurs, blending their trading aptitudes with sensible socialism, and, in Mary Ann's case a touch, at least, of feminism.*

Mary Delany (née Granville)

Mary Delany was born in Wiltshire in 1700 and brought up by her uncle at Longleat House. At the age of eighteen she was married off to an aged Cornish squire, and after his death in 1724 went to live with the Stanleys, earls of Derby. In 1731 she made her first visit to Ireland and began a voluminous correspondence with her sister, Anne Dewes. In 1743 Patrick Delany, a clergyman and author, proposed to her and was accepted. She moved to Ireland and shared his home at Delville, near Glasnevin, Co. Dublin. Through her family influence her husband, already Chancellor of St Patrick's Cathedral in Dublin, secured the Deanery of Down. She was closely involved in most aspects of Irish society, many of which she related to her sister in her letters. After her husband's death she settled in London, where she died in 1788.

HIGH SOCIETY IN DUBLIN

Because of her connections, both ecclesiastical and aristocratic, Mary Delany was in the very heart of Dublin society, and in this letter to Anne Dewes she describes the events of thirty-six hours in that society.

DUBLIN, 25 NOVEMBER 1731

Monday being St Cecilia's day it was celebrated with great pomp at St Patrick's cathedral. We were there in the greatest crowd I ever saw; we went at 10 and staid till 4; there is a fine organ, which was accompanied by a great many instruments, Dubourg [leader of the viceroy's musicians] at the head of them; they began with the 1st concerto of Corelli; we had Purcell's Te Deum and Jubilate; then the 5th concerto of Corelli; after that an anthem of Dr Blow's, and they concluded with the 8th concerto of

47

Corelli. Perhaps you think this was entertainment enough for one day; pardon me, we are not here so easily satisfied as to let one diversion serve for the whole day and we *double and treble* them.

Lord Montjoy [Thomas Windsor] made a fine ball for the Duke and Duchess of Dorset and their retinue, our house was among the invited people, and Monday was the day fixed on. After our music we returned home, eat our dinner as expeditiously as we could, and by seven (the hour named) we were all equipped for the ball; Mrs Graham, Miss Granville, and Miss Usher called on us, and we all went away together, nobody was admitted but by tickets. There was four-and-twenty couple, 12 danced at a time, and when they had danced 2 dances, the other 12 took their turn. No lookers on but the Duchess and Mrs Clayton, who thought it beneath the dignity of a Bishop's wife to dance.

The Duke danced with Lady Allen (the Duchess had the headache) Lord Mountjoy with Lady Caroline [Sackville], Mr Coot with Lady Lambert, Capt. Pierce with Mrs Donellan, and Mr Usher with me; the rest were people you don't know at all; Index [admirer of Anne Granville's] would not condescend to dance more than minuets.

Before the dancing began, the company were all served with tea and coffee; at 9, every lad took out his lass. At 11, those who were not dancing followed the Duke and Duchess up stairs to a room where was prepared all sorts of cold meats, fruits, sweetmeats, and wines, placed after the same manner as the masquerades. We eat and drank as much as we liked, and then descended to make way for the rest of the company. Mrs Clayton went away at 12, the Duchess soon after that, and Phil and I staid till 1, and then with much difficulty made our escapes, the rest staid till 4 in the morning. On the whole, the entertainment was more handsome than agreeable, there being too much company.

The next morning we rose at 9 o'clock, put on our genteel dishabille [dress], to the Parliament House, at 11, to hear an election determined: the parties were Brigadier Parker the sitting member, and Mr Ponsonby the petitioner, Mr Southwell's interest was the first, and the last was Sir Richard Mead's. I believe we were the most impartial hearers among all the ladies that were there, though rather inclined to Mr Southwell's side, but the cause was determined in favour of Sir R.M.'s. I was very well entertained there. Our cousins were also there.

About 3 o'clock Mrs Clayton went home to dinner with her Bishop; we were stout, and staid. Mr Hamilton, a gentleman I have mentioned to you, brought us up chickens, and ham, and tongue, and everything we could desire. At 4 o'clock the speaker adjourned the House 'till 5. We then were conveyed, by some gentleman of our acquaintance, into the Usher of the Black Rod's room, where he had a good fire, and meat, tea, and bread and butter. Were we not well taken care of? When the House was assembled, we re-assumed our seats and staid till 8; loth was I to go away then, but I thought that my kind companions were tired, and staid out of compliment to me, so home we came.

A VISIT TO WICKLOW

In this letter to her sister, Mary describes a visit to Co. Wicklow, starting at Mount Usher, where her friends the Ushers had established a notable garden – it is still famous today.

MOUNT USHER, 21 MAY 1752

Now you must follow me into the county of Wicklow. Mr Usher sent a chaise and a saddle horse for Mrs Donellan, her maid and Gran. D.D. and I travelled in our own chaise and the day being fair Don. rode part of the way. We set out from Delville about 8; passed through Dublin and a most pleasant country, till we come to Bray, (in the *neighbourhood* of which town *Bushe was born and bred*, the place called Cork). We did not stop till we came to Loghling's Town, eight miles from Delville, a very good inn, pleasantly situated; there we alighted to look about us, and bespeak our dinner for next Saturday. From thence we went to Kilcool [Kilcoole, on the coast], where we dined; I can't say much of the pleasantness of the country to that place, only a very fine view of the sea and good road; from Kilcool the scenes are more enlivened and extremely pretty – enclosures, fine meadows, shady lanes, one side skirted by mountains and hills of various shapes, diversified with cultured fields, bushes and rocks and some wood; on the other side a beautiful prospect of the sea, and the roads like gravel walks, the hedges enriched with golden furze and silver May. This country is particularly famous for arbutus (the strawberry tree) and myrtles, which grow in common ground and as flourishing as in Cornwall. Myrtles are so plentiful that the dishes are garnished with it, and next Xtmas the gentlemen in this neighbourhood are agreed to adorn Wicklow church with myrtle, bay and arbutus, instead of ivy and holly. I tell them it is well I am *not* to be *one* of their congregation – I should be tempted to commit sacrilege! The arbutus bears fruit and flowers (like the orange tree) at the same time, and is in its full glory about Xtmas; the berries are as large as the duke cherry and of a more glowing scarlet, the surface rough like a strawberry; I believe you have never seen it in perfection, which makes me so particular in my description of it. I can show you a draught [sketch] of one in perfection done by Mrs Forth Hamilton.

We arrived at our journey's end between five and six, called 24 miles, would measure 36 English. By the name I suppose you think this an exalted situation; *toute au contraire* it is as low as Bradley and hid with trees and hills. The house is a very good one, old fashioned, convenient and comfortable, the hall *very large*, in which is a billiard table and harpsichord, and a large desk filled with books; within it a large parlour where we dine; and within that a drawing room, but the spacious hall and the amusements belonging to it make us give it the preference to all other rooms: the bedchambers are proportionally good to the rest of the house, and excellent easy beds; everything though plain perfectly clean, like the Master and Mistress of the place, who were bred up in Dublin and used to a great deal of company; but a large family – four daughters and three sons, (now men and women) and prudential reasons made them retire and settle down in this place about sixteen years ago, where they have lived a quiet philosophic life and brought up their children extremely well. The eldest daughter is married to a *worthy clergyman*, the second lives with her: they are now gone to the south of France for Mr Edgeworth's health and this morning Mrs Usher shewed me a letter from Mrs Edgeworth, written in a very find hand and a very sensible, agreeable account of the place they are in; the eldest son is bred up a squire at home (their estate is but a moderate one) he is a modest dull sort of youth. The eldest of the two daughters at home seems to be *the housewife* of the family, the youngest plays very well on the harpsicord, and sings surprizingly, though she has hardly ever been taught; they are both very modest well-behaved young women, neither pert nor awkwardly bashful. Our entertainment is suited to the rest – excellent and good things, *well drest* in a *plain neat way*. And now, having given you an account of the country, the people and manners, I must give you rest till the weather permits me to say something of the environs. The chaise is ordered to carry us this morning to the Murrah, a strand two miles off, and whilst it is preparing I must thank you for your charming letter, ending the 14th of May.

The chaises came and we went to the Murrah. The weather was hazy and rainy which eclipsed greatly the beauty of the prospects. The Murrah is seven miles long by the seaside: I think it may more properly be called a terrace than a strand, as it is not even with the sea, but raised by a gentle slope, the turf as fine as any well-mown garden walk, between that and the sea, when the tide is out, is a strand covered with pebbles some of which are very beautiful, like the Scotch pebbles.

As we drove up the Murrah we had a view of the town of Wicklow, which lies close to the sea, and spreads on the side of the hill; a point of land makes a bay, and there is always some sort of shipping which enlivens the prospect. On the right there is a great variety of agreeable views of fields, gentlemen's houses, gentle hills, and towering mountains. One very remarkable circumstance belonging to the Murrah I forgot to mention which is that it is situated between the sea and the lake; the part we went over was about three miles, the lake continued all that way and runs into the sea at Wicklow Town. To make you comprehend it better than you can by this awkward description I send you a little scratch not worthy to be called a sketch.

We got home a little before dinner; the rain was so violent I could not gather any pebbles; so on Friday morning I got up at six, took one of the young ladies who drove me in a one-horse chair, her brother was our squire, and to the Murrah we went again. The day was clear, and I gathered several pretty pebbles and got home again by breakfast: as soon as breakfast was over we all set out except Mrs Donellan and Mrs Usher, in chaises and on horseback and went to the Devil's Glen, called two miles off, but will measure four.

The Glen is somewhat like Longford's and has all the horror but not the beauty. We went to the top and looked down into it; we could not go in our chaises above a mile, the rest of the way we walked and went on truckle-cars, part of the way was too steep and rugged for any carriage.

When we had satisfied our curiosity and looked till our heads grew giddy, we returned; but before we got home went to a place called Cronerow Rock belonging to Mr Eccles, a gentleman who lives in Glassnevin: the rock grows like a great wart on the top of a very great ascent, the whole hill is feathered with a fine young oak wood, and the rock is so mixed with woods in some parts that you can only see it through the trees. We climbed very nearly to the top of it with some difficulty and fear of stumbling among the loose pieces fallen from the rock; but I could have spent a whole day in picking up the fragments, some glittering like diamonds, others like fine marble – I never saw so beautiful a rock. I wish I had an enchanting wand and could by a stroke place it just beyond my brother Granville's fine cascade. There are several natural caves in it, and the wood, which continues from the utmost top of the rock quite down to the valley, by so good a taste as his might be made the finest thing I ever saw; but by this robbery could I effect it, I should indeed do great injury to one of the prettiest countries I ever saw in my life. When you are on the summit of the hill I have described, the prospect is charming and terminates with the Murrah and the sea beyond it. I have seen nothing in Ireland so beautiful but it is more owing to nature than art.

I saw several places worth taking notice of, but if I did I should send you a book instead of a letter, so I return to good Mrs Usher's house, where after a very good dinner we went to Mr *Tighe's*, Rosanna [Rossannagh] by name whose garden is divided from Mr Usher's by a very pretty clear river: he came in his boat to *waft us over!* It is a very pretty place and house, neatly kept, and capable of great improvement, which he is setting about with all speed. He went to England for six weeks, saw

PainsHill, Mr Charles Hamilton's and Wobourn Lodge, Mr Southcote's and now says his own place is hideous and will pull it to pieces! His ground lies finely, his trees very flourishing; a river bounds his garden, and the fields and country about him lie very advantageously to his view.

We left Mount Usher on Saturday morning stopped at Loghling's Town where we had bespoke our dinner and whilst it was getting ready walked about. Mr Danville has an estate and seat just by the inn, the house old and ruinous and ingeniously situated to avoid one of the sweetest prospects I ever saw. There is a natural terrace on the side of the hill where the house stands, of about a mile at least; the part I saw of it is a gradual descent from that to the highway, but at such a distance as not to incommode you either with noise or dust; part of the bank is quite green, and smooth like a slope in a garden, the rest covered with shrubby wood or fir-trees. Across the valley where the road runs, is a river over which is a bridge and a bank divided into fields with little cabins; hedges and trees rise on the other side, overtopped with mountains, whose deep purple made the verdure of the nearer prospects appear to great advantage. Mrs Don. who had never been at this place to consider it before, says if she can bring Mr Danville to any terms (he always lives in England) she will *build a nest* for herself *there*.

Letters from Georgian Ireland: the Correspondence of Mary Delany, 1731–1768, The Friar's Bush Press, Belfast (1991)

Ann McCracken (née Joy)

Ann McCracken was the youngest child of Francis Joy who, in 1737, had established the *Belfast News Letter*. As an expression of her independent and practical outlook she also set up a small milliner's shop in Belfast which she gave up on her marriage to Captain John McCracken, and devoted herself to rearing their six children (the eldest had died in infancy), one of whom was Henry Joy McCracken, another Mary Ann.

A MOTHER'S SOLICITUDE

After the arrest and imprisonment of Henry Joy for his activities with the United Irishmen, Mary Ann had gone to Dublin to visit him in Kilmainham. Despite the fact that at this time Dublin was at the height of its brilliance and wealth, Mary Ann had no inclination or time for socializing. Her solicitous mother in Belfast sensed this and wrote the following letter to Mary Ann.

NOVEMBER 16TH, 1796

Dear Mary

I wrote your sister the 14th but as I got a Frank I thought you would be glad to hear from us as often as possible. I was sorry to find by John's letter to his wife that you dont like Dublin tho' I was sure it would be the case, but I hoped your seeing Harry and that perhaps you might get some of your Muslins sold would partly reconcile you to it – there was five taken up yesterday and sent to Carrick on a bald woman's Oath – Joseph Cuthbert, Tom Storry . . . and O'Donnell Clarke and Tom Stewart and a sadler. This day there was a poor man in fever stole out of his house and went through this street calling out a Republick for Ireland and he was a Republican, he had a hank^f tied about his head and as pale as Death. In a few minutes he had after him a great multitude of soldiers – when I looked out our window I saw a little Officer put his hand to his sword and [order] him to hold his tongue. They carried him to the Guard house when to their great mortification they found the man deranged of a fever. John does not mention anything about Mr Bunting, indeed his letters are so short they are not satisfactory. Our friends here are all very attentive to me and I could do pretty well about your business if I had money to give the weavers and indeed they behave very well. I hope you will try to see as many places as you can while you are in Dublin, and tho' the times are not so pleasant as we could wish them I hope they will mend and I have found, what I thought to be distressing, turn out for good and we should always trust in Providence that can bring good out of evil. I saw Miss Templeton today, they are all much the way you left them. The Miss Tombs drank tea with us tonight. Poor Ellen Holmes is very ill they think its the measles. Pray let us hear from you, I thought when you left this I was to hear from you very often –

All the family joins me in affectionate complements to our friends at Kilmainham and to you and John and Peggy and Mr Bunting

and am

Dear Mary your affectionate mother

Ann McCracken

Mary McNeill, *The Life and Times of Mary Ann McCracken*, Blackstaff Press, Belfast (1988)

Mary Ann McCracken

Mary Ann McCracken was born in Belfast in 1770, a daughter of Captain John McCracken and Ann Joy. Although delicate as a child she 'received the same extensive education as young gentlemen'. When she was barely out of her teens she and her eldest sister Margaret established a small muslin business, in which Mary Ann took responsibility for the office functions. In the 1780s and '90s there was widespread dissatisfaction with a political situation in which, of the 300 members of the Irish House of Commons, only 72 were freely elected, and the Catholics, then forming 90 per cent of the population, were not represented at all. The French Revolution of 1789 was celebrated in Belfast with great enthusiasm and in 1791 the first Society of United Irishmen was established in Belfast, involving not only Wolfe Tone and Thomas Russell, but also Henry Joy McCracken – Harry, Mary Ann's favourite brother. This involvement led, almost inevitably, to the arrest of Henry Joy in 1796 and his subsequent fourteen months in Kilmainham Jail; his continued involvement with the United Irishmen, culminating in his defeat at the battle of Antrim, led to his recapture and his public execution in 1798. Mary Ann herself lived until 1866.

TO HER BROTHER IN KILMAINHAM JAIL

In this, the first of her surviving letters to Harry after his arrest and
detention in Kilmainham, Mary Ann reveals herself as a feminist – long
before the term was invented. She also shows herself to be a caring sister,
reassuring her incarcerated brother, a little injudiciously to modern eyes,
of the disposal of 'a certain article'.

MARCH 16TH '97

Dear Harry

Since I wrote last I could find but another opportunity, and not liking
the mode of conveyance did not take advantage of it, you are not
therefore to suppose, that the silence of your friends is owing Either to
indifference or neglect but merely to want of opportunities. We were very
uneasy about you for some time but are happy to find by the accounts
that you are getting better. John is just arrived and delights us all by the
agreeable intelligence he brings us of your mended health. There cannot
be more extraordinary Revolutions in Politics than what have taken place
of late in the minds of many people here – a Ci-Devant Major of the
Belfast Volunteers and a Cousin of our own told Frank last night that a
friend had shewed him the United Irishman's test, that he approved highly
of it, and would not have the least objection to take it, as he had done
more violent things often before. Whether this is the effect of fear or
conviction I shall not pretend to determine, but it is very evident that since
the people have appeared to be the strongest party their cause has gained
many friends, some of them I suppose from conviction . . . . A certain
article which was the only cause of uneasiness to you at the time you were
taken up, was concealed in the house till the late strict search which has
been made about town, and not daring to keep it any longer, we gave it in
charge to a man in whom we had confidence, who buried it in the
Country, so that its being found can't injure any person. The black men
have been visiting some houses in town last night and, taking arms out of
them, and it is generally thought, that ere long we will be out of the King's

peace, the General here says that he will put us under martial law directly. There were six prisoners brot to Town this evening, for refusing to swear allegiance and came undismay'd singing Erin go Brath. It would equally please and surprise Mr. Russel to hear that a certain Botanical friend of ours whose steady and inflexible mind is invulnerable to any other weapon but reason, and only to be moved by conviction has at last turned his attention from the vegetable kingdom to the human species and after pondering the matter for some months, is at last determined to become what he ought to have been long ago, Frank proposed him at the last meeting of the society, and I hope his sisters will soon follow so good an example. I am glad John is come home for more reasons than one, John Gordon did not behave as well as possible while he was away endeavouring to frighten Mrs McCracken, by telling her, that he would make John suffer when the revolution would commence and always praising McIlveen at John's expense, but what was still worse, he beat the servant maid one night when Mrs McC. was in our house, and hurt her so much that she had to be bled and was very ill for several days. I mention this as I understand he is high in confidence.

I have a great curiosity to visit some female societies in this Town (though I should like them better were they promiscuous, as there can be no other reason for having them separate but keeping the women in the dark and certainly it is equally ungenerous and uncandid to make tools of them without confiding in them.) I wish to know if they have any rational ideas of liberty and equality for themselves or whether they are contented with their present abject and dependent situation, degraded by custom and education beneath the rank in society in which they were originally placed; for if we suppose woman was created for a companion for man she must of course be his equal in understanding, as without equality of mind there can be no friendship and without friendship there can be no happiness in society. If indeed we were to reason from analogy we would rather be inclined to suppose that woman were destined for superior understandings, their bodies being more delicately framed and less fit for labour than that of man does it not naturally follow that they were more peculiarly intended for study and retirement, as to any necessary connection between strength of mind and strength of body, a little examination will soon overturn that idea, I have only to place the McCombs, Val Joice and our worthy Sovereign opposite to Mr. O'Connor Mr. Tone and our dear departed Friend Dr. Bell (three little men possessing much genius) to show the futility of such an argument. But to return, is it not almost time for the clouds of error and prejudice to disperse and that the female part of the Creation as well as the male should throw off the fetters with which they have been so long mentally bound and conscious of the dignity and importance of their nature rise to the situation for which they were designed, as great events at least display if they do not create great abilities I hope the present Era will produce some women of sufficient talents to inspire the rest with a genuine love of Liberty and just sense of her value without which their efforts will be impotent and unavailing, their enthusiasm momentary as a glittering bubble which bursts, while it rises, and as every discarded affection leaves a damp and melancholy void in the mind where it has been once entertained, so those who are flaming for liberty today without understanding it (for where it is understood it must be desired as without Liberty we can neither possess virtue or happiness) may perhaps tomorrow endeavour to damp the ardour and cool the courage of others when they begin to reflect on the danger which they incur and the little advantage which they derive from it. I do not hold out the motive of interest as an inducement for man to be just, as I think the reign of prejudice is nearly at an end, and that the truth and justice of our cause alone is sufficient to support it as there can be no argument produced in favour of the slavery of woman that has not been used in favour of general slavery and which have been successfully combatted by many able writers. I therefore hope it is reserved for the Irish nation to strike out something new and to shew an example of candour generosity and justice superior to any that have gone before them – as it is about two o'clock in the morning I have only time to bid you goodnight –

Believe me
Yours affectionately
Mary

FEAR, SUSPICION AND INTRIGUE

After her brother's first arrest for his involvement with the United Irishmen, Mary Ann wrote to him in jail to describe to him the events in Belfast. It should be remembered that at this stage Napoleon was leading his victorious armies across Europe and the ports on the other side of the Channel were filled with fleets poised for invasion. Ireland was a crucially weak point in England's defences.

APRIL 13TH 1797

Dear Harry,

I recd yours by J. Haffey, and have still to regret your being so much hurried that your letters are neither so long or particular as we could desire. On Friday night last there was a search made in John Alexanders by Col. Barber, the high Constable etc. and a society of United Irishmen consisting of twenty-one members who were in the house at the time taken up, James Burnside and another weaver of Johns and one of ours were among them, and they are all confined in the Artillery barracks, fortunately for Alexander and his son they were not at home at the time and have kept out of the way since. Two boxes were broke open one of which belonged to Mr. McCabe and it is said there were some letters from Mr. Russell to him in it, and in the other there were five guineas which they also carried off with them, it is supposed Newell* the painter was the informer and that idea seems to be confirmed by what happened last night. John's family were knocked up about twelve o'clock and as soon as the door was opened the whole party rushed upstairs to J. Gordon's room (who has left John some time ago) they were conducted by a little man dressed as a cavalry officer with a handkerchief tied across his mouth who everyone of the family instantly recognised to be Newell, having seen him there frequently with J. Gordon. He went directly to a hole in the floor under the bed which Gordon had showed him before, but fortunately

* A notorious spy.

there was nothing in it but a little hay. John invited them to search the rest of the house which they refused and would only examine the yard, and they looked above the cowhouse where had formerly been some guns, but found nothing. Jackson, who was tried along with Hart, and J. Haffey are both taken up, also Butcher another of Cuthbert's foremen, Kane and Templeton of the Star Office, together with many more whose names I dont know. Your old friend Owen Burn who had sworn against B. Coile was the man that was hanged at Omagh ten hours after he had committed a robbery. It is supposed that the prisoners here will be taken to Carrick tomorrow to be tried and I am happy to hear that all the United Irishmen in Derry have been acquitted.

Remember us as usual and believe me to be
Yours affectionately
Mary Ann McCracken

A person called on Frank a few minutes ago to tell him that Wm was taken up, he was in a tavern with two others when that same little villain Newell came in disguised as he was last night and pointed him out, and familiarised as we now are to such incidents it would scarcely affect us were it not for the present situation of his wife. She does not yet know it and I do not know how she may bear it.

FRUSTRATION AND INDIGNATION

After Thomas Russell, one of Henry Joy's associates in the founding of the United Irishmen, had been arrested, there were aborted plans for his escape – foiled by his removal to Downpatrick Jail – and frenzied efforts to raise money for his defence. Mary Ann was deeply involved in this, contributing heavily herself. She had planned to visit Russell in prison and had mentioned this to Mr Teeling, an old friend of the family, who thoroughly frightened Mary Ann's mother, thereby deterring Mary Ann from her proposal. In frustrated rage Mary Ann dashed off this letter to her 'dear enthusiastic friend' Eliza Templeton. Her state of mind is shown by the fact that the letter is not merely unsigned but unfinished.

My dear Eliza.

I was never so completely vexed and perplexed in all my life as at present owing to [an] absurd and ridiculous indescretion in mentioning my intention to Mr. Teeling never supposing it possible that any person would think of opposing what I considered so natural and so much my duty. I should have . . . but no matter. It is an injury I can never forgive from whatever motive it proceeded to have my liberty of action confined and circumscribed, had Mr. Teeling kept his advice for my own private ear, or communicated his opinion on the subject to no one else but my sister I could have easily have brought her over as I have already, but not satisfied with that he had mentioned it to Frank and called himself just as I was at breakfast. I cannot however blame him altogether for introducing the subject as Frank first mentioned it, and after I had prepared my mother by despising cowardly friends and various other preliminary conversation – Mr. Teeling got her completely intimidated by his plausible arguments of involving the family of my Father, Mother, Brothers. Etc. the house being marked and numerous other absurdities, that she had declared her determination that if I do go her and I should part for ever, not that I would attend to that silly threat, only as it shows the degree of fear she labours under. I am not certain that I should [cause] her serious uneasiness without a probability of doing some real good. I am just at a loss what course to pursue, but this I know that I will henceforth renounce all such cowardly friends and shall take particular care never to hold any confidential communications with anyone of that family again, or give them an opportunity of influencing my conduct by their maddening officiousness, but in the present instance of what use are these determinations. I know of no other course I can pursue than writing by Mr. Ramsey tomorrow to know if it be possible to do any good by going, and if so to defy all prohibition. I hate such half measures, but I know not what I ought to do – farewell. I do not ask your advice because I know you would not wish to give it and yet I would like to have it – only this I know that the greatest enemy I could possibly have could not have caused me the same degree of uneasiness that a professed friend has done whom I wish now that I had never considered as such –

HER BROTHER'S LAST REQUEST

Just before his public execution – ironically on land that had been presented to the city by his great-great-grandfather – Henry Joy had requested his loving sister to write to Thomas Russell, telling him of the circumstances and manner of his death. Incredibly, despite her grief, the very next day she carried out her dear brother's request.

BELFAST, 18TH JULY 1798

In obedience to the last request of a much-loved brother, I write to you who were his dearest and most valued friend, to inform you of the interesting but affecting particulars of his death, which took place yesterday in pursuance to a sentence of Court Martial by which he was found guilty of being a leader of the Rebel army in the battle that was fought at Antrim on the 7th of June last, though the witnesses who swore against him contradicted each other in some material points and one of them declared the other, who was the same man that swore away poor Storey's life, to be a man of infamous character, and not deserving of the smallest credit. I should have informed you as perhaps you do not see the public papers, that he was taken on the 7th instant along with 2 or 3 others by two of the Carrick yeomen, a mile or so from that town, and depending on a pass that had been procured for him in a feigned name he did not think of making his escape till it was too late, he and his companions being unarmed and having no means of defence whatever. I am thus particular because he has been accused of cowardice in suffering himself to be taken at all tho' he had no possible means of resistance. He was committed to Carrickfergus Jail where he was closely confined in a cell until Monday morning last, when he was brought up to Belfast and lodged in the Donegall Arms which is now a prison, from which he was removed in the afternoon to the Artillery Barracks, his trial came on yesterday at 12 o'clock at which I was present that I might bear testimony to his conduct which was cool collected and composed during the whole day, he took notes of the trial and remarked on the contradictions of the witnesses, but at the same time was certain of being convicted, as the trials here are mere matters of form, not one having been yet acquitted. I was also present when he received his sentence and was ordered for immediate execution, at which he neither changed countenance nor colour, but still retained his usual cheerful composure, for though he wished to live to serve his friends and his Country yet he was resigned to die, on being asked if he wished for a Clergyman he said he would be glad to see Mr. Kilburn who was accordingly sent for, and in the meantime as Dr. Dickson was confined in the same prison he requested to have his company which was also granted, with whom he conversed with firmness and ease, he said he was now vexed at having been angry at those by whom he had been cruelly treated, one of them in particular and from whom he would never have expected such conduct, not content with perverting Henry's words in excuse for his own base desertion, he even attempted to blacken his character by accusing him of crimes which he never either committed himself nor suffered others to do on whom he had any influence.

Mr. K. when he arrived was so overpowered by his feelings that it was a considerable time before his tears and sobs would permit him to utter a short prayer, after which as the time was short I began to take off a little of Harry's hair to preserve it for a few of his friends, when Major Fox entered to order him out and told me I might save myself the trouble as the General had ordered him to take it from me, against this I remonstrated but in vain, he would take it from me by force if I did not give it up which at Harry's request I did, who reminded me of what was true that it was but a trifle. – I accompanied him to the place of execution, where I wished to remain to the last, but even that small consolation was denied me. I was forcibly torn from him as they said by the General's orders and should have made more vigorous resistance, but Harry requested me to go and I feared disturbing his mind in his last moments by such an unequal contest – I have been told since that when I left him Major Fox came up to ask him for the last time, an offer of pardon having been made before trial some time if he would give any information, at which he smiled and told Fox he wondered what reason he had for supposing him such a villain but as they were now to part forever he would shake hands with him – I was also informed that when he ascended the scaffold he attempted to address the people but the noise the horses made was so great that he could not be heard. A few minutes put him beyond the power of oppression, but robbed his friends of a treasure never in this world to be recovered – never did I see him look so well so interesting or seemingly in such perfect health as that day and the evening before, notwithstanding the hardships he had of late undergone being mostly exposed to the open air and sleeping frequently on the cold wet ground and enduring difficulties of every kind – it is some small consolation that even his enemies were forced to admire his conduct both from what they say and from the evidence by which he was convicted, he acted like . . . [torn] . . . the last and smiled when the rope was put about his neck. I was allowed . . . [torn] . . . of embracing his lifeless corpse on condition of interring it before dark and the numbers in that short time who crowded in to weep over it, showed how much he was beloved. It was as impolitic as cruel to murder one who was the idol of the poor, he who was so patient of injuries, so benevolent of heart, hundreds now pant for revenge whom he had the power and benevolence to restrain, but this could neither restore him to life nor would it gratify him if he was sensible of it.

At the same time that he desired me to write he bid me to vindicate his friend Mr. Richardson's character from the unjust suspicion which had been cast upon it by his fellow prisoners and for which the testimony of a dying man who had been his most intimate friend will surely be sufficient.

I have been thus minute because it is probable we may never meet again, as Frank intends leaving this unhappy Country in a few days and the rest of the family mean to follow him as soon as he can prepare a place of refuge in some distant land where we may in peace cherish the remembrance of him whose loss we must ever lament, whose memory will be always dear to us and whose virtues we will still admire and revere. At the same time we should endeavour to be resigned to the will of that Being who overrules and directs all things, and who would not suffer us to be afflicted but for some useful purpose. That the cause for which so many of our friends have fought and have died may yet be successful, and that you may be preserved to enjoy the fruits of it, is the earnest wish of one who remains with the truest regard your sincere friend

Mary Ann McCracken

A LETTER NEVER READ BY ITS RECIPIENT

It is generally accepted that Mary Ann McCracken was in love with Thomas Russell. It is, therefore, particularly poignant that while it arrived with Russell before his execution, he deliberately did not read it 'lest it disturbed his mind'.

I hoped to have had the pleasure of seeing you once more but as that satisfaction seems now improbable I feel most deeply at the disappointment, not that I supposed your mind required the support of any human consolation, possessing as you do that comfort which the world can neither give nor take away – but I wished to have assured you of my intentions of continual friendship to your sister & also to request if there are any others who have claims on your affection, that you will not thro' motives of false delicacy scruple to mention them that those who shall ever venerate your memory may know how to show it that respect of which it is so truly deserving – it is impious and certainly cruel in us to repine at the prospect of your removal from a world every way so unworthy of you, yet it is impossible to divest oneself so entirely of selfishness as not to feel the deepest regret for the loss society will sustain in being deprived of one of its most valuable members – a firm reliance on the wisdom and goodness of that Providence that governs the universe & who does not permit afflictions in vain, can alone reconcile us to such a melancholy event – if there is anything I can do either now or hereafter that would in the least degree contribute to your satisfaction you cannot gratify me more highly than by naming your wishes – I have no doubt but that the day will arrive when your loss & such as yours will be universally deplored even by those who are at present most active against you. May I request that you will indulge me with another lock of your hair, that I received already & for wh. I am particularly obliged I had to divide with my sister & my friend Eliza, each of us shall preserve our [torn] invaluable treasure as a memento of virtue seldom equalled & worthy of affection [torn] of imitation. Forgive me imposing so long on your so very precious time, [torn] to be considered worthy of your friendship is an honour which we shall ever most highly value. I am joined by my sister in every sentiment of attachment & veneration.

I remain,

Yours most truly,

M. McC.

THE WELFARE OF WORKERS

Although this letter to the newspaper that had been founded by Francis Joy in 1737 is signed 'A Subscriber', it is generally agreed that Mary Ann McCracken was its probable author. It exhibits precisely the sort of views that might be expected of one of her background and sentiments.

MAY 17, 1803

To the Editor of *The Belfast News-Letter*

Sir,

Actuated by a sincere regard for the happiness of my fellow creatures, I am induced through the medium of your valuable paper, to address to the Proprietors of Cotton Mills, and other Factories, the following hints, which from long experience have been found conducive to the preservation of health and of morality:–

The passage, stairs, floors and inner doors should be constantly kept clean, by sweeping, washing with soap and water, and scouring with sand, the walls whitewashed once a month, especially during summer, and for those parts most likely to rub off, the lime should be mixed with skim milk.

The above operations appear best adapted for destroying effluvia or miasmate, the concommitant of all crowded rooms.

Quicklime should daily be thrown into the houses of Convenience attached to large factories, which will effectively destroy all *fetid effluvia*, and produce a most valuable manure. As much air as is convenient should be allowed into the rooms both day and night, and particular attention should be paid to the cleanness of the workers' hands, faces, etc. who ought to be provided with warm coats and cloaths so as to be protected against the evil effects of wet and cold, when going to and returning from their work; sufficient time should be allowed for amusement in the open air during fine weather, especially after the dinner hour.

A very serious responsibility attaches to those who employ children, for if the morals of children become depraved, from what sources are we to procure virtuous men and virtuous women? Those, therefore, who draw children from the superintending care of their parents, ought to consider themselves as accountable for their conduct, consequently very circumspect in the choice of their overseers, and in the men and women employed with the children; keeping the sexes as separate as possible, offering premiums and every other source of encouragement for good behaviour, discouraging improper conduct, by levying fines for swearing, obscene expressions, etc., and holding out such inducements as will procure a strict attendance at Sunday Schools.

In short the proprietor of a Factory is in duty bound to consider himself as the parent of a numerous family, and to do all those things which a sensible and virtuous parent would do; for it is obvious that nothing short of such conduct will prevent *emaciation, ignorance*, and *vice*, or e'er long the following exclamation – *Live Morality! – Perish Factories!*

I am, Sir, etc.

A Subscriber

Mary McNeill, *The Life and Times of Mary Ann McCracken*, Blackstaff Press, Belfast (1988)

THE EARLY
NINETEENTH
CENTURY

One of the welcome additions to the stock of Irish women's letters in the early nineteenth century is the appearance of letters from an emigrant, in this case Mary Cumming, a daughter of Revd Andrew Craig, minister of Lisburn Presbyterian Church and, therefore, quite literate – as, indeed, her letters show. In 1811 she had emigrated with her new husband to Virginia. Her letters, one describing the crossing of the Atlantic and her relief at setting foot on land, and the other describing the death of her baby daughter, touch virtually all the emotions – the extreme discomfort of the ocean crossing, the vision of a new world and then the devastating tragedy of the death of her new-born child. Her ability to communicate – though she had no literary aspirations – is impressive.

A woman who most definitely did have literary aspirations was Maria Edgeworth. Her father, Richard Lovell Edgeworth, was quite a remarkable man. In addition to marrying four times, he found the time to interest himself in such diverse subjects as bog reclamation, road construction and, as a good Irish landlord, estate management. He encouraged his daughter Maria and collaborated with her in writing Practical Education *and* Essays on Professional Education. *She published*

The Parent's Assistant *in 1796, before engaging herself in the writing of fiction. Before she wrote the letters presented here she had written the well-known* Castle Rackrent *in 1800, followed by* Belinda *in 1810 and, in 1809, the first series of* Tales of Fashionable Life. *She thus had considerable experience of literary achievement, which shows only too clearly in her writing.*

The reverse is true of the Brontë girls, whose literary achievements postdate the samples of their letters reproduced here. Their father, Revd Patrick Brontë, born near Loughbrickland, Co. Down, had literary aspirations and had a 'slender output of poems and stories'; The Maid of Killarney, *published in 1818, two years after the birth of his eldest daughter, Charlotte, was a tale of love between an Englishman and an Irish Catholic peasant girl. While the Brontës would never be described as Irish writers, having an Irish father gives them every claim to be represented as Irish women.*

Mary Cumming (née Craig)

Mary Cumming was one of the daughters of the Revd Andrew Craig, minister of Lisburn Presbyterian Church. In 1811 when she was only twenty she married William Cumming of Armagh, and went with him to America, where he was a cotton merchant in Petersburg, Virginia. She never really recovered from the death of her child; she herself died in 1815, never returning to her beloved Strawberry Hill, the family home outside Lisburn. Her letters were mainly to her sister Margaret, with whom she enjoyed a particularly close relationship.

TRANSATLANTIC CROSSING

In this letter to her sister Margaret, undated but apparently written on 8 November 1811, Mary describes her voyage across the Atlantic to her new home in Virginia, with her new husband William, whom she refers to as 'Mr Cumming'. Her description of what to her was still a 'new world' is refreshing.

Thank God, my dearest Margaret, I have the happiness of telling you that we got safe to New York yesterday about three o'clock. It would be impossible almost to conceive the delight I felt when again I set my foot on land, I never in all my life felt so truly grateful to Providence. Oh, my dearest friends, I never imagined when I last wrote to you what a voyage across the Atlantic was! But let me endeavour to give you some account of our passage.

This day six weeks we left Liverpool, and I may say I never had one day's good health since that time. We did not sail till Saturday morning as the wind was not fair. I was confined to my bed for three weeks – the longest ones I have ever spent. The sickness was most dreadful, it was with difficulty I could rise for a short time in the evening to get my bed made. There I lay, not able to lift my head from the pillow. My dear Mr. Cumming attended and nursed me during all my illness with the greatest care and attention, in fact he did everything for me that it is possible for one to do for another. For a long time he had to feed me like a child, indeed I was quite as helpless as a infant. As long as I live I shall never forget his attention and kindness. I was so weak at last that nothing would remain in my stomach, and for some days I lived almost on port wine and water. Our passage (except for a few days) was very rough, indeed it blew a constant gale, alias a storm, for most part of the time. When we got near to the banks the weather became warm and pleasant for a few days. I then got better and was able to be on deck for the most part of the day. I then enjoyed myself very much, the weather was very warm, unpleasantly so for a short time, but I shall never be a good sailor, I suffered more the last Sunday we were at sea than any day before. But I have dwelt long enough on the miseries of a sea voyage, let me think if it has any pleasure to make amends for them. That question would require some consideration.

I was very much delighted looking at the sun setting, which is a glorious object at sea. I believe I only saw it set three times during our voyage. I remember one night in particular watching him sink into the ocean, the scene was delightful. For a great length of way waves appeared fringed with burnished gold, the sky was so clear and the air so pure and reviving that it wanted nothing but a little bit of terra firma in view to complete the scenery. Fine as the scene was I thought as I stood admiring it 'It would be a far more delightful sight to see him set behind an Irish mountain.' When shall I see that again?

Our accommodations were very good, we had plenty of most excellent provisions, and what was our greater comfort, there was a very good cow on board, so that we had plenty of good milk, which is the greatest luxury at sea you can imagine. Our party was very pleasant. There were two ladies on board, one the captain's wife, the other a very pleasant woman who lives in Augusta. Mrs. Brown is just as bad a sailor as myself, for some days we would not be able to go from one room to the other, but I will not think any more of our troubles. Mr. Cumming was not once sick, which was a great blessing, I think he looks fatter and better than when he left England. I have often amused myself thinking when at sea if the author of the miseries of human life had ever crossed the Atlantic. If he had, I think it would have afforded him a few more. For instance when you are lying in bed in a rough gale of wind trying to get a little sleep, the ship to roll in such a manner that you have to hold yourself in bed in order to prevent being heaved on the floor, or when you would attempt to stand to come smack against the side of your bed so that your legs would retain the impression for a fortnight after. All this happened to your humble servant. There was one night I thought we were all gone, and I bawled out stoutly, as you may imagine. But I almost forgot to tell you I have had the felicity of seeing the sea in a storm, I went on deck one evening for the purpose, but I was very glad to get down to my room again. You cannot imagine a more grand and awful sight. The ship was lying quite on her side, the waves now and then dashing over her, sometimes she would get between two of these great mountains of water that you would be almost sure would swallow her, then rise to the top and plunge down in a sea of foam. I never wish to witness so frightful a scene. Our captain said he never had so rough weather even in the middle of winter. We passed several ships on the way, and had the satisfaction of getting before them all. The 'Lydia' is a very fast ship, we have often made ten miles in a hour, which is going pretty quick. Last Monday morning I heard the enchanting news that land was in sight. This is the most delightful hearing that can be imagined. The pilot came on board soon after, and we were all sure that we would get up that night, but the wind got into a very bad humour and left entirely, so that we were obliged to spend another night at sea, in sight of the smoke of New York, which was very provoking to be sure. During the night we got within ten miles of the shore, and the next morning the wind took it into its head that we should go no further that day, but we did not agree with Mr. Boreas, for we thought we had been quite long enough in his power, so we got a boat and here we are all safe landed in the great city of New York. In my life I never was so enchanted with the view of the shore and the harbour coming up. I can give you no idea of the beauty of the

American woods at this season of the year. I have often admired the colouring of the trees in the Autumn, but never could have conceived that the colour could be so much richer here than with us. The green is so very bright, and I can compare some of the woods, to nothing but groves of gold; and the nice little white wooden houses peeping from among the trees render the scene altogether the most captivating that I have ever looked at. Then we had a fine view of the fortification and spires of New York. Oh, how I wish you had been with me, I am sure you would have been as much pleased as I was.

We dined yesterday at an inn, Mr. Robert Dicky came to see us as soon as we arrived, and insisted that we should all come to his house and stay with them, so we got here yesterday evening. Mrs. Dicky is a cousin of Mr. Cumming and Mr. Brown, she is daughter of Dr. Brown of Baltimore. I believe Mr. Dicky is a very rich man, I never saw so elegant a house as this is, everything in it is superb. I am writing in a splendid drawing-room, there are so many fine things to look at that I can hardly write for admiring them. I have just been in the parlour. There is to be a party of gentlemen here today, the dinner table is laid out in great style, indeed I wish it was ready for I begin to feel my land appetite again. Mrs. Dicky is a very pleasing and accomplished woman, I like her very much. Her mother is with her at present, I believe she will go on to Baltimore with us. I think we shall stay a few days here, I have not seen much of it yet, but what I have seen I like very much. The trees along the streets have a good effect, they consist chiefly of poplars that look beautiful just now. I have been almost all morning writing this sad scrawl, but I know my dear Margaret will excuse it, for indeed I am not myself yet. You would laugh to see me walk, I feel as if I was still on shipboard.

Oh, my beloved friends, how anxious I am to hear from you again! I think I shall get a letter from you on my arrival at Petersburg, I will write immediately after I get there. We think of staying a day or two at Philadelphia, and three or four at Baltimore. Mr. Cumming wrote to Armagh to-day. I hope Mary Cumming is with you now. When you write tell me all the news you can think of. The weather is rather cold here at present. I must reluctantly bid you farewell as my head begins to ache.

Write, my dearest Margaret, whenever you receive this. Do not disappoint me for I am very anxious to hear how you all are. Give my kindest love to my dearest Father and James and Rachel. I suppose James has gone to Dublin. I hope my Father will write to me sometimes. You will not have to complain of my neglect, for it is the greatest pleasure in the world for me to write home. Give my kindest love to Miss McCully and my dear Meg, I hope they are both well. How often I thought of you all when I was ill. You never in your life saw me so thin as I am at present, but I expect to get fat directly. I must go and dress for dinner.

> Farewell, my dearest Margaret! Write soon to
> Your Ever Affectionate
> Mary Cumming

THE DEATH OF A CHILD

In this letter to Margaret, Mary tells of the death of her child; one of her sisters, Arminella, had died at the age of six.

NOVEMBER 17TH, 1812   BLANDFORD

I never before felt reluctant to begin a letter to my beloved Margaret, for never till now had I bad news to communicate. Oh! my dear sister, how you will be grieved to hear that God has been pleased to take to Himself my darling child. The little angel breathed her last on the fourteenth September, and 'winged her early flight to heaven.'

When I look back on the last three months it appears to me like a frightful dream. I dreaded this Fall, but little did I think we were to experience such sickness as we all have done. I was taken with a bilious fever about the middle of August, which confined me to bed for three weeks, during my illness my sweet infant took a bowel complaint, from which she never recovered. This is the most dangerous disease that children have in this country, my beloved child lingered in it for three weeks, two physicians attended her, but all would not cure her. Oh, dearest Margaret! it almost breaks my heart when I think that my lovely

75

baby is gone forever. Oh, that you had seen her, you would not wonder at my sorrow. She was one of the most beautiful infants I ever beheld, and so good, she was too good to stay in this troublesome world. I believe she knew me, for when I would go to take her out of her little crib-bed the darling would look up at me and laugh, she was beginning to take notice of everything, but she is an angel in heaven, and in that happy place I trust in God I shall meet my little Mary.

It will be long before I can get the better of her loss, for I am so lonely without my sweet pet, but I will try all I can to be resigned to the will of Providence.

> 'The numerous ills of life to prove
> To us survivors may be given,
> My babe has scaped this gloomy train,
> And winged its early flight to heaven.'

These lines I think of very often, they are the last verse of the beautiful little poem my dear Father gave to my Mother on the death of Arminella, I brought them with me. My dear William has suffered very much as well as myself this Fall, he had the same kind of fever that I had which confined him for a long time. He is now, thank God, almost quite well, he walks to Petersburg every day. I am getting better every day though still very weak. I was not sufficiently careful of myself after my first illness and was taken ill again and with one complaint and another have been confined to my room for nearly three months, but we now have fine, cold, frosty weather, which will soon bring us round again. I now know too well what ague and fever is. This has been among the most sickly Falls ever known in Virginia. I do not know from what cause. The physician that attended me told me he visited from thirty to forty patients every day in Petersburg. A lady who lived near me this Fall lost two fine children in less than a fortnight, but there have been very few deaths among grown-up persons. This is a sad, unhealthy climate, but I have had my seasoning, as they call it, and hope not to be ill again during my stay in this country, which I trust will not be very long, for oh, I long to breathe once more my native air in darling healthy Ireland. It is the country for me. They talk of the wetness of the weather, but what matters when the people have no agues and fevers? I do not know what I should have done during my illness if it had not been for Mrs. Freeland, a lady of my acquaintance who lives very near me. I never experienced so much kindness and attention from a stranger as I have done from her at the time poor William and I were so much distressed that we could do nothing. She came here, ordered everything to be done that was necessary, and indeed appeared more like a kind relation than an acquaintance.

She came every day to see me, till she herself was taken ill, but is now almost recovered, she spent Sunday evening with me. Dearest Margaret, how you would love her if you knew her. Mr. Freeman is a Scotchman, they have two fine children, both girls, the eldest (Agnes) is a great favourite of mine, she is fifteen years old, just about the age of my darling Rachel. She is very fond of me and brings her work and sits with me very often. When I get well she is coming to stay some time with me. Whenever I would say to my dear Mrs. Freeland how much I felt obliged to her for all her kindness I am sure she would reply 'You would do the same for me if I were in your country.' I can never forget her uncommon attention to me. When, my beloved Margaret will I receive another letter from you? I have not had one this long long time. Your last was dated 28th May. I am sure you have written several since that time but none have come to hand. I would have been very uneasy had I not heard by a letter from Mary Cumming that you were all well. William had one the other day from Mr. Cumming dated August, in which he mentions that the Strawberry Hill people were all well. Still I am most anxious for a letter from yourself. My beloved Margaret, what would I give to see you and all the dear dear inmates of Strawberry Hill once more. Will the time ever come that I shall be with you all again? I trust from my heart it will. My affection for you increases every day. God bless you, for if anything happened to you my happiness would be gone for ever. I think as you do that there never were sisters loved each other as we did and do. I have great reason to be thankful, for I enjoy a thousand blessings and that first and greatest of all is having the best of Husbands, which I have. My dearest William is my constant comfort and support through all my trials, he is so kind and indulgent to me that now I feel quite lonely when he goes even to Petersburg. You would require to be in the house with him to see all his kindness. God bless and spare him to me. He is very busy overseeing his labourers every day and getting the garden put into nice order. This is a sad stupid letter but my spirits are not good. Will you tell my dear Father that I wish he would write to me soon. Give my affectionate love to my dear friends in Armagh. Tell Mary I am very much obliged to her for her kind letter which I will answer when I am better able than at present. I hope my darling James and Rachel are well. I am rejoiced to hear my dear Father is in such excellent health. Long long may he continue so!

William joins me in the kindest love to you all, and wishing you every happiness, I am my darling Margaret's ever affectionate,

M. Cumming

It is William's opinion that the war cannot last long, the great majority of people of information and property are for peace. God grant that we may soon have matters settled. I forgot to mention in my last letter that I had made inquiries respecting the young man of the name of Morrison that my Father mentioned, but I cannot hear of any such person teaching school in Petersburg. Write to me dearest Margaret, whenever you receive this and let your letter be very long. I wish you would send your letters to Liverpool directed to the care of William Brown and Co. and they would send them by the first opportunity. William has received several lately from that place. I suppose Miss McCully has left Lisburn long before this, I hope she and Margaret are well. When you write give my most affectionate love to them. I intend to keep myself constantly employed as I can this winter, for thinking much does me a great deal of harm.

Oh, my dear Margaret, will you and I ever wander about Strawberry Hill and talk of the days that are gone? I trust we shall, I will write soon again when my spirits are better. You have got the picture by this time, I suppose. I hope you will think them like, once more, farewell! my darling sister.

ed. Jimmy Irvine, *Mary Cumming's Letters Home to Lisburn*, Impact-Amergin, Coleraine (1982)

Maria Edgeworth

Maria Edgeworth was born in England in 1767, the third child, by his first marriage, of Richard Lovell Edgeworth. It was not until 1782 that she moved with her father to the family estate at Edgeworthstown, Co. Longford. Her early writing was encouraged and influenced by her father. In 1800 she published her first novel, *Castle Rackrent*, the earliest regional novel in English, which was an acknowledged influence on Sir Walter Scott. Her *Tales of Fashionable Life* were published in 1809 and 1812. In later life she was much engaged in famine relief; indeed her last novel, *Orlandino*, published in 1848, was written for the Poor Relief Fund. She died in 1849.

KEEN OBSERVATION AND LUCID REPORTING

After the publication of the second series of Tales of Fashionable Life *in 1812 Maria's father was very anxious to take Maria to London to benefit from her fame. In 1813 the opportunity arose and they set off. In this letter to Mary Sneyd, her father's sister-in-law, whom she called 'Aunt Mary', Maria tells of the first part of their journey to London.*

WEDNESDAY, 31 MARCH 1813   BANGOR FERRY

I will go and write a few lines of a letter to my dear Aunt Mary and – Oh why should you write *now* my dear? You have nothing new to tell her. Nothing new – but I love her and wish to write to her and if I did not love her I should be worse than Caliban. Well write only a few lines. That is just what I mean to do, and to go on with my letter at any odd place where we *stop the night*.

Honora will tell you all we saw at Howth, so I go on from Holyhead. Breakfasted with Mr. Grainger who was so agreeable that my father disordered a chaise on purpose to go on in the mail with him. This mail coach very comfortable held but four inside, so we were all to ourselves.

My father says he never received so much pleasure in his life from any eatable as from a china orange which Mr. Grainger gave him just at the moment when his mouth was parched with thirst. This orange quite recovered him from the remaining effects of sea-sickness and then he was ready to converse and to enjoy this gentleman's conversation. I wish you had heard him speak of Sophy Ruxton. He says she is the most agreeable, sensible, charming young woman he has seen in Ireland. He declared he was quite enchanted with her and bid me tell her so. If he had not lived abroad he never would have ventured to speak with such enthusiasm. He says he shall go to Paris and he will I am sure do all he can for Lovell. He has lived in good or at least high company abroad – Prince de Neufchatel – Berthier – and the D'Arembergs – told us a variety of entertaining anecdotes. Caulaincourt now duc de Vicenza was brought up in the family of the Prince de Condé – l'enfant de la maison the playfellow of the Duc d'Enghien. Bonaparte employed Caulaincourt to seize the Duc d'Enghien and the wretch did so and has been repaid by a dukedom. We asked how the present Empress is liked in France. 'Not at all by the Parisians. She is too haughty – has the Austrian scornful lip and sits back in her carriage when she goes through the streets.' The Parisians used to make these complaints against Antoinette. On what small things the popularity of the high and mighty depend. Mr. Grainger thinks there will soon be a counter revolution in France.

Josephine is living very happily and amusing herself with her garden and shrubberies. It is a curious circumstance that this cidevant Empress and Kennedy & Co the London nursery man are now as Mr. Grainger says in partnership. She had a license to send him what shrubs and flower seeds she chuses from France and he has license to send her cargoes in return. Mr. Grainger saw great cargoes arrive from him. I dare not go on with more of his anecdotes lest they should fill all my paper. He seems a most good natured benevolent *shrewd man of the world*. He will carry over Madame Recamier's box for me and is glad to do it as M. Recamier has obliged him. We parted from Mr. Grainger at Bangor Ferry and were very sorry for it. He went on in the mail. He will see us again in London. I wrote to my aunt Ruxton this morning to say we had met Mr. Grainger.

At Bangor Ferry at the inn door we saw a most curiously packed curricle with all manner of portmanteaus and hats slung in various ingenious ways – behind the springs two baskets, the size and shape of Lady Elizabeth Pakenham's basket – A huge bunch of white feathers sticking out from one end of one of the baskets as we approached to examine out came the live head of a white peacock – a Japan peacock – On the other side a Japan peahen. The gentleman to whom the carriage belonged appeared next carrying on a perch or stand made to fasten behind the carriage a large fine macaw! The servant who was harnessing the horse would not tell to whom the carriage belonged. He always replied to all enquirers 'It belongs to that there gentleman'. An impertinent vulgarian with his chin buried in a figured yellow handkerchief went on saying 'Its the most *curous* concern ever I *seed*. I should a'thought it belonged to the Marquis of Sligo for he's the most curous man I know in all England. Only for the horse in't good enough for he.' We have not been able to settle whether the master of this equipage is a gentleman – a gentleman's gentleman or a shewer of wild beasts but my father is decided he is a man of no literature as he had never heard of Miss Edgeworth or her works.

N.B. My father has left directions with Francis Beaufort about the part of patronage that is to come to Dublin from Dr. Beaufort and also proper instructions about the trunk.

Tomorrow we go to the slate quarries spend morning there and sleep at Capel Curig. Good night. I am perfectly well – not the least tired – have enjoyed this fine day – had a delightful walk before dinner in a hanging wood – by the water side – pretty sheep paths – wood anemones in abundance with their white flowers in full blow – two ploughs going in a field below the wood – very chearful – the sound of the Welchmen's voices talking to their plough horses. The plough giving the idea of culture and civilization contrasted agreeably with the wildness of the wood and mountains.

We shall be at Dr. Darwin's Shrewsbury on Saturday – Good night again.

Thursday. How fortunate we have been as to the winds and weather. Last night was a violent storm of wind and thunder and lightening. This morning all was bright and after a breakfast of muffins 'very good and very hot too' we set out for the slate quarries. Stopped at Mr. Worthington's nice neat house the front of which is all slate plaistered over so as to look like beautiful stone. Mrs. Worthington received us hospitably and spoke in high terms of Sneyd and William. Sneyd she said was a most amiable youth and William 'no doubt was a young man of great talents'. She added Mr. Worthington's opinion that he would certainly succeed in the world. Mr. Worthington to our disappointment was not at home; he is at Liverpool. With Mrs. Worthington was visitor a Mrs. Waterson, who had got up at 5 o clock this morning, or some morning lately, to read Vivian. My father of course liked her much. We proceeded to the slate mills; in our way saw the inclined planes and little carts full of slates running down. Tell William that we were much pleased with the sawing mill – particularly with the screw and wheel which keep the saw down upon the blocks of slate. I will not here attempt to describe any of the machinery to you; but I *trust* I have the principal parts of it by my fathers clear explanations fixed in my memory. Tell William we saw the cutting engine and saw the men splitting the slates and took our time, full time to see every thing quite at leisure. The road to the slate mills is most beautiful. It goes by the side of a glenn at the bottom of which is a stream flowing over such rocky and uneven ground that it forms a continued cascade. The rail ways are above six miles long. They are very narrow; I had formed an idea of their being much more *magnificent*; but it seems that in this country canals and rail ways are made as useful and as little splendid as possible. I was surprised to see the rail ways winding round the rocks and going over heaps of rubbish in many places where you would think a wheelbarrow could scarcely go. We went on from the Mills to the slate quarries. We had been admiring the beauty of landscape and the sublimity of the Welch mountains, my father did not say anything to raise my expectations, but when we arrived near the place he took me by the hand and led me over a hill of rubbish of slates on the top of which was a rail way. We walked on till we came between two slate *mountains* and soon found ourselves in the midst of the slate quarries. It was the most sublime sight of all the works of man I ever beheld. It is like a mine above ground. The height of slate rock on each side of the *terrace* on which we stood appeared to me about 70 feet and below us thirty feet deeper we saw men at work quarrying. The men looked like pigmies in the midst of these vast works. There is a curious cone of greyish colored slate which the workmen say is good for nothing, but it is good for something. It has a sublime and picturesque appearance. Mrs. E has made a sketch of it. We saw one man with a great wooden mallet at one stroke break a mass of slate in two as large as the tea table and as thick as the great bible. While we were in the quarry (I was going to say the *mine* for it is more like a mine than a quarry) a heavy shower of hail came on which falling between the rifts of the rocks and blown by the high wind added to the sublimity of the scene. We were comfortably sheltered in one of the slate sheds in which the workmen sit to split slates. Upon the whole I was much more pleased than I had expected. I was actually silenced with admiration of the sublime both in nature and art. I was astonished that *art* could appear sublime in the midst of the sublimity of nature. Forgive me aunt for turning up here.

Finding that Mr. Worthington is at Liverpool my father has decided to go to Liverpool so we shall write to say that we cannot be at Derby or Byrkley Lodge on saturday or tuesday. We have come on to Conway at which place I now write. We proceed to Holywell and Chester. I said the weather had been favorable to us but I forgot to tell you that during the storm of last night it snowed just enough to cover the tops of the Welch mountains with white to encrease the beauty of the prospect for us. They appeared more majestic – strong contrast of bright lights and broad shades – the foreground all green – the *leaves* of the honeysuckles all green in the hedges and fine hollies bright green – primroses in abundance. It was literally 'Spring in the lap of winter'. We stopped at beautiful Aber where there was the prettiest landlady I ever saw with a beautiful sister – eat bread and butter and cheese and excellent pancakes tell Lucy. Quite refitted set out on a delightful sunshining evening to pass Penmaenmawr. My father says that the mountain has considerably altered its appearance since he knew it first – from the falling of masses of rock and the crumbling away of the mighty substance. Cultivation has crept up its sides to a prodigious height. In parts seemingly inaccessible there was pasture. A little cottage nestled just under the mountain's huge stone cap. The fragments of rock that have rolled down, some of them across the road are ten times the size of the rock in Mr. Keating's lawn and in contrast to this idea of danger are sheep and lambs now feeding quietly – the lambs not larger than kittens. One of them I particularly remarked was no larger than little Francis's poor deceased *Muff* or *Tippet*. Neither my father or Mrs. E ever went over Penmaenmawr in the evening, so that they had never seen it with the western sun upon it and it appeared quite new to them.

We got to Conway in excellent time, 6 o clock in the evening. Mrs. Rous the landlady of the Harp inn recollected my father, Lovell and my aunt Ruxton. She is a nice looking old woman – very like the old mother in the print of Robin Gray. The boy to whom Lovell used to be so good, and who stopped my father the last time he went over Penmaenmawr to tell him that Lovell had given him Lazy Lawrence, was drowned: he was one of many lost on the Ferry boat at Conway in a great storm 5 or 6 years ago.

The old harper who used to be the delight of travellers at this inn is now sitting in an arm chair in the little parlor within the kitchen in a state of dotage. His harp stood in the room in which I slept carefully buckled up in its green cover. At Bangor there was no harper. The waiter told us they were 'no profit to master and was always in the way in the passage so master never let none come now'.

In the midst of all the sublime and beautiful I saw this day I had also a happy mixture of the comic for we had a Welch postillion who entertained us much by his contracted vocabulary and still more contracted sphere of ideas. He and my father could never understand one another because Mr. E called *quarry* quarry and the Welchman called it querry. And continually the Welchman asked us the burthen of all he said 'if we would not like to be driven to Caernarvon'.

Friday morning. 7 o'clock dressed and ready to go on with my scribbling. Before I go on I must assure you my dear kind Aunt Mary that it is a great pleasure, not the least trouble to me to write this letter.

I write at odd minutes when the horses are changing – after breakfast and after dinner for a quarter of an hour at a time. You know it is impossible that should tire me. It is worthy of observation to me at least that all my present conveniences for writing, which are all that any lady can want [are] gifts of various Sneyds. I use Miss Sneyd's pocket inkstand which has been of continual comfort to me. My ivory cutter penknife is a gift [from] Aunt Charlotte and my little Sappho seal a present of aunt Mary's. I keep them all with the letter I am writing in the ridicule* Fanny made for me which never quits my arm and has been, tell her, the joy of my life.

Now to go on with our journey – 8 o clock a fine morning walked down to Conway Ferry – The great archway under Conway Castle covered with wall flowers in *full* blow – Very pleasant crossing the ferry. The beautiful view of Conway Castle and the country near it, which has been drawn at least a thousand times, we could not help wishing to be able to draw again just as we now saw it. I said to one of the boatmen, 'You Welchmen have a beautiful country to live in'. 'Yes Ma'am but I wish I was out of it.' 'Where else would you wish to be?' 'With the armies abroad Ma'am where I once was.' 'With whom? – and where?' 'With General Moore Ma'am at Corunna.' 'What did you think of General Moore?' 'I thought he was a brave man and I liked him.' My father then continued the conversation and as I was going ashore I heard only the concluding sentence which was framed as ingeniously for his purpose as any lottery advertisement could be. 'I wish I had some of the dollars we was obliged to throw away at Corunna or one even or a part of one even for I was overworked last night and almost done up but if I had sixpence I could set myself up again with a pot of porter.' My father gave him the sixpence which you will allow he deserved. In our way from Conway to St. Asaph nothing new. In our way from St. Asaph to Holywell we past a beautiful gateway of Wyatts belonging to a Mr. Hughes. Mrs. E took a sketch of it. We went in to look at the prettiest Porters lodge I ever saw – two neat old women who shewed

---

* An alternative word for reticule.

us the inside. Nothing could be more comfortable except that the kitchen fire smoked. 'Ah Madam,' said the old woman, 'these chimnies that be made for beauty do seldom draw well.'

She was a very cheerful old woman but I would not change our own good Margery Woods for any porter-ess in Christendom. My father inquired where the iron work of these gates was made and hearing that it was made at Hardinge a town a few miles further on he stopped there. It soon afterwards began to snow very hard but we stopped nevertheless at the Iron founderies at Hardinge and tell William we wished very much for him to see the boring engines and the punching machine. My father said, 'If my little Francis was three years older I should wish for him. If I live what pleasure I shall have some time in shewing him these things.' As I do not think my Dear Aunt you would wish for details of all I saw even if I were capable of giving them clearly, I will not expatiate but only note that I hope William will hear from the best authority a description of the punching machine with its perpendicular *oval* wheel. My father is to write to this foundery about his iron gates.

Have you had any snow? We had a heavy shower of snow for two hours. The snow was very obliging to us for it came in a part of the country where we had little to see. Even through the snow however we spied the green gooseberry bushes in every cottage garden in full leaf. It would be worth while to plant gooseberry bushes if only for the pleasure of seeing this earliest green bush of the spring. The white thorn – I mean the black thorn is in leaf in the hedges and for miles we have seen such beautiful hollies in the hedges! I wish my aunt Charlotte would be so kind to take a few small hollies out of Wilkinsons garden and have them planted in the new ditch between Woods and Duffy's also some cuttings of honeysuckles and some cuttings of pyracanthus. Enough can be had from my garden. I wish she would ask Deniston to repair the dashing of Connors house.

Adieu my very dear Kind aunt Mary I must finish abruptly – post going – I have been as happy and well as possible.

Maria E

Fashionable Life

In this letter to Frances Maria Edgeworth, the eldest daughter of her father and Frances Beaufort, and her favourite sister, Maria describes some of the 'fashionable life' she was enjoying in England.

Monday, 31 May 1813

My dear Fan –

While my father and mother are gone out to buy some colors to paint a scene for Mrs. Marcets play, which is to be acted tomorrow I am allowed to have the pleasure of writing a tiny note to you in a frank which my mother intended to fill.

Without preface I will begin with what is freshest in my memory – the history of yesterday. Went at 11 o clock to pay a visit to Lady Wellington, who had sent to beg to see us – sat a delightful half hour with her. Her little boy is getting quite well. Tell Sophy Ruxton I asked if there was any print of her children. She said 'There is none but if there was one I would certainly send it to Miss Ruxton.' There is a pretty little *drawing* of them *designed* not drawn by herself – one boy riding on a cushion and the other standing beside him and trying to draw a sword from the scabbard. This was in the exhibition last year and Lady Wellington thinks that this gave rise to the report Sophy heard of there being a print. The more we see of Lady Wellington the more we both admire and love her and the more comparisons we make with others the more we feel her easy, graceful superiority – but no more about her, or I shall forget every body else. At one o clock went with Madame Achard and M. Dumont to Kensington to pay a visit to a Mrs. Mallet, whose voice, and conversation were so strikingly like Mrs. Tuite's that my mother and I could hardly wait till we got downstairs to say so. I need not tell you that we thought Mrs. Mallet very agreeable. Went to Kensington gardens but a shower came on and all the dressed groups were forced to take shelter under trees and parapluies. Everything unfortunate is picturesque. Nevertheless I was sorry it rained. Madame

Achard is a clever, rich, benevolent Swiss lady with a screeching voice which my father cannot endure. Tell my aunt Mary that M. Dumont is very plain, very fat and as far from sentimental as any human being can be. Au reste he has in conversation all the abilities his letters promise. He is an excellent critic, full of anecdote – entertaining and instructive – Just a French homme de lettres laid out for that kind of life – The mornings spent in writing and reading – dining out regularly. For the last 4 years it is said he has never dined at home. He has been very friendly whenever he has met us, but from his disliking crowded parties and our happening to be engaged on the days when he was invited to dine at the same places we have not seen much of him. I do not think he will ever come to Ireland though he still says he will. He seems to have bound himself for ever and ever to Bentham.

After our return from Kensington my father and Mrs. E paid a visit to Dean and the Miss Allotts and after various tickets had been left at various doors, which I forgot to mention, we dressed for dinner and went to dine at Lady E Whitbreads. Tell Sneyd I quite agree with him in thinking her agreeable – perhaps the more so because she was uncommonly attentive to us. The company were Sir H and Lady Davy – Mr. and Mrs. Ponsonby – Mr. Freeling – Mr. Brougham – Mr. Rogers (Pleasures of memory) – *and* Sheridan. Sheridan came in late – sat next to Rogers, who was sitting next to me – whispered to Rogers and made him tell *who* every body was; then bid him introduce him to me and stretching across said 'Mr. Rogers has used me very ill and Lady E Whitbread has broke her compact with me, for I had bargained that I should sit next to Miss E'. Mr. Sheridan conversed a great deal both with my father and with me, with the ease and freedom of a man who had no character for wit to sustain. He looks bloated but his eye is an eye of inextinguished and inextinguishable fire – dark, very prominent, more like the eye of an ostrich than of a man. Some say it is very alarming; but I did not feel it so. Indeed I always think it less alarming to talk to persons of the first abilities, than to fools. The fools are always trying to shew their wit by finding faults. People of abilities are in general more indulgent and better able to balance accounts. Tell my aunts that Mr. Sheridan talked to me much of Mrs. Honora E who, as he said he had heard was the handsomest woman of her day and he had heard that she bore some resemblance to his first wife – Miss Linley, whose picture by Sir Joshua Reynolds is now in the exhibition. I do not see the resemblance. Sheridan seemed to *feel* whilst he spoke of his first wife. A gentleman told me that he saw him go into the exhibition room after all the company had left it one day lately to look at her picture. He talked of Miss Seward and Major Andre &c.

After dinner when the ladies went upstairs Lady E Whitbread shewed us her house, which is both magnificent and *comfortable* 4 large rooms on a floor and a delightful boudoir and below a library looking into a garden. Company in the evening – Miss Grant a friend of Anna's – Lord and Lady Grey – *both* very agreeable – an old dowager Lady Grey – Lady Asgill her sister Mrs. Bouverie (agreeable) Miss Ogle in a fur cap sister in law to Sheridan – Miss Berrys – Mr. Atkins and two or three *persons unknown*. The party not being too large it was very pleasant – broke into small conversation groupes sitting and standing. Lady E Whitbread said 'There is no chance you know of Sheridan's coming up till one o clock.' But lo! he made his appearance before eleven, took a little stool and sat down in the middle of our group consisting of Lord and Lady Grey Mrs. Ponsonby and Mrs. E. The stool cracked under him so he was forced to take a chair, but his elevation did not make him the less agreeable. I don't think he had drank up to his wit-point, but he was perhaps much the more agreeable to ladies. The moment he came in, Lady Elizabeth whispered to Mr Whitbread 'Order supper soon, and plenty of punch, for Sheridan will want it'. We were very sorry we could not stay to supper. We were engaged to Miss White and after a delightful hour, when we got up to go Sheridan held us back and said 'You are not going, you *must not go*'. But alas we were in duty bound to go away so we went, and Miss White was much obliged to us for the sacrifice we made. There we found a crowd of people – among them Mrs. Opie Lady Crewe and a Mrs. Broderip, whom I mention for future description – Lady Asgill (again) and her sister Mrs. Wilmot who came and had waited an hour on purpose to be introduced to us. My aunts will recollect *who* Mrs. Wilmot is – the lady who modelled the cow for Lady Holte – She appears to me by far the most sensible of the family . . .

. . . As I have more time than I expected I will go back my dear Fan to some of our last week's operations and mention our interview with Mrs. Inchbald tho' I rather think my mother has already written you all an account of it. With much difficulty Mrs. Morris a friend of hers prevailed upon her to come so far into the world again as to dine at her house to meet us (Then Alas we were engaged). But we went in the evening – found the rooms absurdly crowded – as thick as pins in a pincushion – made our way through pinioned forms to a recessed window where at last we saw the waving black plumes of Mrs. Inchbalds bonnet. The recess was dark and till I pushed fairly into it I could see no more. She was in black and muffled but well dressed for effect – a tall commanding figure much handsomer face (as well as I could see) than I expected – prodigious fire and expression in her eyes and whole countenance – A theatrical yet not an affected manner (or at least affectation became natural) – quick feeling and the same originality and openness and carelessness about *committing* herself – and confidence in the sympathy of others – the same freedom from pride that apes humility and the same frank readiness to praise and to be pleased which appear in her letters to us. She talked a great deal (for our gratification) about the Simple story and told us that the price she had been originally offered for it was Oh shameful! Oh incredible – *two* guineas! How my aunt Mary will lift up her hands and eyes! . . .

Your affectionate sister

Maria Edgeworth

ed. Christina Colvin, *Maria Edgeworth: Letters from England, 1813–1844*, Oxford (1971)

DINNER ANECDOTES, TREES AND SHRUBS

In this letter to her mother Maria attempts to cheer her up by relating some dinner anecdotes and follows with a description of a pleasant walk in the grounds.

My dearest Mother

... After having written so much on business it is time I should think of something to amuse you my dearest mother and to draw a smile if I can from the dear breakfast table. *Who* is at it? Only Mamma – Lovell and Sophy? Or are the young ones all returned from Black Castle? I may safely say I love you *all* whoever you be. Now let me see – What shall I tell to win a smile from you all?

Lord Lansdowne shall win it for me. Among the many pretty little anecdotes he used to give me when I sat beside him at dinner he told me one of his own childhood. It was brought out by my observing that children had very early a great desire to produce an *effect*, a *sensation* in company and that when they see that they have made a change in any grown person's countenance even if they do not know the cause they are delighted and persist if not from *malice* from curiosity and a desire to try and experiment and see what will happen.

Yes said Lord Lansdowne I remember distinctly having that feeling and acting upon it once in a large and august company when I was a young boy. It was at the time of the French revolution when the French nobility began to emigrate and among the first the Duke and Duchess de Polignac came to England and with all their suite came to Bowood where my father was anxious to receive these illustrious guests with all due honors. One Sunday evening when they were all sitting in state in the drawing room my father introduced me and I was asked to give the company a sermon. I had a little time given me for consideration and then I began. The text I chose – quite undesignedly was '*Put not your trust in Princes*'. The moment I had pronounced the words I saw my father's countenance change and I saw changes in the countenance of the duke and duchess de Polignac and of every face in the circle. I saw I was the cause of this and though I knew my father wanted to stop me I would go on to see what would be the effect and I repeated my text and preached upon it and made out as I went on what it was that affected the congregation.

Afterwards Lord Shelburne desired him to go round the circle and wish the company a good night. But when he came to the Duchesse de Polignac he could not resolve to kiss her he so detested the patch of rouge on her cheek. He started back – Lord Shelburne whispered a bribe in his ear '*I'll give you a shilling*'. No – he would not – and they were obliged to let him off and to laugh it off as well as they could – his father very much vexed. The duchesse de Polignac not a woman as Lord Lansdowne observed accustomed to have her advances slighted or her kisses refused was somewhat surprised at the event and I suppose set it down to the account of English rusticity – bien anglois!

Another days dinner anecdotes – We were talking of Glenarvon and I said we had thought the Princess of Madagascar – Lady Holland – the best part of the book – so good that we fancied it had been inserted by a better hand. Lord Lansdowne said 'It is certainly written by Lady Caroline Lamb and she was provoked to it by a note of good advice from Lady Holland. At the time when Lady Caroline Lamb knocked the page on the head with the hearth broom and when he was in imminent danger of dying in consequence of the blow and her Ladyship obliged to hide herself waiting the event, she wrote to Lady Holland who was at that time high on her list of friends. She wrote to thank her for having as she heard defended her on this occasion against the world's abuse. Lady Holland answered that she had indeed defended her Ladyship by positively denying the whole story as she never had believed one word of it till she was to her astonishment assured of its truth by Lady Caroline's own note. She added that she advised Lady Caroline in her then dreadful circumstances to think less of what the world said and more of the pain she had given her mother by her conduct and of the *horrible risk she had run*. This incensed Lady Caroline to such a degree that she immediately went and wrote the Princess of Madagascar.'

When I said we thought the book stupid and that we could hardly get through it Lord Lansdowne said that unless from curiosity to know what would be said of particular people he was not sure that he could have got to the end of it. 'But' added he 'besides this *natural* curiosity about my friends and acquaintance I expected to meet myself and to find myself abused for just at that time I had given her Ladyship sufficient provocation according to her manner of judging. I met her, to my sorrow one morning at the corner of some street where there was a great mob – I think at the same time of somebodys election. She was riding, I was walking. She jumped off her horse – came up to me took me by the arm and declared I should carry her through the mob to Sir Francis Burdett who was in some house at the farthest end of the street – But I positively refused declaring it was quite impossible.' Another time there was a set of gentlemen met on Sir S Rommily's election committee she would go to it tho no other woman was to be there and tho she was told there would be a mob. Lord Lansdowne met her there and remonstrated. She made her way up to a poor tame sheepish looking old curate 'Reverend Sir you shall protect me! Under your protection what harm can befall me. I am sure you will protect me' and she fastened upon his arm and walked him up and down till his heart was like to break. Another time she went to a quaker meeting –

But Francis calls and says I *must* come out to walk and that he hates foolish letters . . .

half after 4

Returned from a pleasant walk – on the gravel walk with Francis. Though it had rained torrents all morning 5 minutes sunshine had made the walk quite dry – it is so well made – rounded like a bed well tucked-up. Francis has shewn us all the varieties of trees and shrubs which have been stowed into this small compass and which he now has revealed to view – The tulip tree and acacia and variegated oak and the varieties of maple and ash and the variegated rhododendron and Chinese dwarf elm and all that you and Fanny may remember seeing here *and* he abused old Black at every turn – especially for leaving *two* leaders instead of one to his trees, thereby occasioning them to fork and rot . . . I wish I had time to write to Harriet. As for Lovell I both love and admire him and I recommend to him 'Report of the minutes of the evidence before H of C on Education' – price 15 shillings. It contains much that will interest him on schools.

I recommend Harriet and Fanny to read in the third part of Sir W Temples Miscellanea 'A Defence of the essay on antient and modern learning'. It contains a good view of history in small compass. This whole book of Sir W. T's Miscellanea was recommended to me the last evening I spent at Bowood and lent to me to read on my journey by a Mr. Denman a very sensible lawyer – the man who defended the Derby prisoners. Lord Lansdowne brought him in for one of his [? boroughs]. He came the day before we left Bowood. I was very sorry we saw no more of him. As we sat down to dinner hearing me say I was going next day to Mrs. Joanna Baillie's he asked me after her and I asked if she was an acquaintance of his. 'I am proud to say I am a relation of hers and I am proud to say I am a friend of hers.' From this beginning a friendship between Mr. Denman and me soon grew – as high as it could in a few hours. He is brother to Dr. Baillie's wife – only a *connexion*. I wish gentlemen would be accurate. He talked much of Mr. W. Strutt. . . .

Yours affectionately

Maria E

LATE FOR DINNER

In this letter, also to her mother, Maria describes her embarrassment at arriving late for dinner, and explains that this was because their hosts dined at 6 p.m. in the country. She then goes on to describe the house – and her own aversion to an excess of Egyptian decoration.

SATURDAY, 17 APRIL 1819   DEEP DENE

Deep *Dene*   Dene a saxon word meaning a deep rift in a wood – in short a deep dingle

My dearest mother,

Your wish that we should be at Deep Dene is accomplished. We are at last at this beautiful place in this sweet valley of Dorking. Not as we had last year hoped to be, with the great and good Sir Samuel Romilly but still we are with hospitable and kind people and in the midst of all the luxuries of life and all that gilding and painting, and bronzing of Art, can do within, and all that Nature can do with hill and vale, dingle and bushy wood to make the owners and their guests happy.

The first evening of our arrival we were so late that even in driving thro' the vale of Dorking we were in an agony that prevented our enjoyment. We were cross because we were late. The Carrs who are enthusiasts about the beauties of the vale of Dorking and who know nothing of the Hopes but that he has built a great new brick house and pulled down some old house in Chirt park which they loved had spoken with sufficient indignation of the Manufactory looking brick edifice which they say has set the valley on fire. At first sight the offices and the house all irregularly joined with archways and cupolas and strangeness of red brick certainly did strike us as frightful in the midst of a most beautiful country. Our friend the housekeeper and several footmen standing at the arched doorway watching in the dusk for our arrival, and the first words in answer to mine of 'Is it dinner time?' 'Yes Ma'am. Dinner has been waiting this hour' increased my uncomfortable feelings. Fanny was so much tired that we determined she should not go to dinner especially as we heard that Conversation Sharp and some other gentlemen were here. I had taken it for granted that the Hopes dined at the same hour in Town and country. But instead of 7 they dine at 6 in the country and various operations and leaving takings and a visit to Lord – I mean to Lady Carrington had altogether detained us too late in Town. Fanny's health and the pity and interest which it and she excited stood us in good stead. We dressed in the utmost hurry skurry in less than five minutes I am sure made our appearance in the drawing room where luckily the circle were standing and sitting by dim firelight and our guilty faces could scarcely be seen. From the midst two black and white figures whom I knew to be Mr. and Mrs. Hope each with hand extended came to meet us and with one comfortable pressure of each hand set the mind at ease. I descried by the wood fire light the wooden cut of Mr. Sharpe's face and was re-introduced to a Mr. *Harness* whom you may remember tho' I do not. He told me he was introduced to us *first* at Lydia White's just after we had been presented to the (Qy.) Duchess of Sussex. He is an agreeable man and Mr.

Sharp was what they call (and I hate the expression) *in great force* that day and there was an admirable dinner of all manner of well disguised French dishes and creams and soufflés and ices and more than would have sufficed for the dinner of the first bon vivant in Town was sent by the good natured Mr. Hope to Fanny. As soon as I could steal away after dinner I got to her and found her as pale as a turnep wrapped in my shawl. After having swallowed a little jelly she went to bed – a most comfortable French mattress – Canopy bed – large enough for four such as she and I – three rooms opening into one another – small but superbly furnished. I was cross even with the fine furniture that night and regretted the dear Carrs and the home comforts we found there.

I was shockingly afraid that Fanny was going to be ill again *here*. She had but little sleep in the night and in the morning a new misery! Honora wakened with one of her sad sick headaches – Impossible that either of them could think of getting up to breakfast. But there was one comfort. Mr. and Mrs. Hope breakfast in their own room. Only Miss Burrowes (Mrs. Hopes niece) and Mr. Harness were at the breakfast table. This whole first day was uncomfortable as you may guess. But this day all is well and bright and happy. Honora and Fanny are both refitted and we have had charming walks and drives. Fanny first was taken out in a carriage and then had a little walk with Mr. Hope and me – a beautiful walk through *the* deep dene! – Larch and young beech just come out? and grass as green and fresh as Erin's – birds singing – lambs feeding and soft April air everything to delight Fanny going out for the first walk after her illness. She fixed on a beautiful place for a seat which Mr. Hope says he will have there and will call Fanny's seat. Nothing can be more courteously kind than Mr. and Mrs. Hope are to us. I am very glad to see that her looks have improved much within this last fortnight and her spirits are better but she has too little to do too many real good fine things and too much time to think over painful recollections. Her living children are both fine boys and they will in time I hope reanimate her.

Mr. Hope keeps up in my mind the opinion I early formed – not of his taste, for I think his taste is the worst part of his mind, but of his information and general powers of conversation. In a very long tete a tete walk I had with him he gave me a history of the progress of architecture so perfectly clear that it might have been written down as he spoke it and your dear father and Louisa would have admired it and Leslie Foster with all his memory and all his accuracy could have found no fault. The most *entertaining* part of the conversation however was on persons not things. You may judge of the degree of our intimacy when I tell you that Mr. Hope related to me the whole history of his love courtship and marriage and moreover of Miss Berrys courtship of him – disappointment – anger – and quarrel with Mrs. Hope – All of which I must reserve for future fireside conversations. One detached anecdote however I am afraid of forgetting and it is too good to forget.

When Mr. Hope was a young man and Captain in the Marylebone volunteers he was at a city dinner at his Colonels. A young lady sister to the lady of the house sat beside him at dinner. He was shy and she was shy and not a word passed between them during the first course but towards the end of the second the young lady as it is supposed feeling it incumbent upon her to do the honors of her sisters house and to say some thing to the young stranger and recollecting that he was just returned from his travels and that he had been at Constantinople she hummed several times and at last the first sound of her voice he heard in this question 'Pray Sir how many concubines has the Grand Seignior?' Mr. Hope was so entertaining during this walk that it was as much as I could do to enjoy the beauties of Nature. But so beautiful a walk and with such a variety of beauty I never had in my life and my companion judiciously refrained from pointing out beauties or forcing admiration from me. He gently turned or stopped when we came to any delightful point of view but that was all and after a long walk one day he took Fanny and me again over the part which I liked best to shew it to her. Nothing can be more obliging and kind than he is to us. I dare not attempt any description of grounds or country. All I can say is that I hope you will some time see them for yourself and that my present pleasure is incomplete for want of your sharing it my dearest mother and friend. I long also to have my aunt Ruxton with me but one cannot have everything – Tiresome old trueism which meets one at every turn of life.

This house is in its present condition scarcely handsome in its external appearance. The stable at the bottom of the hill looks like a vast square brick manufactory. The house like some of the views in *Athenian Stuart* of Turkish buildings grotesque and confused among trees in no one particular taste and besides flaring in red brick instead of stone or marble. Mr. Hope assures me that many churches in Lombardy in particular that famous church in Milan Santa Maria delle Grazie is of red brick. I am sorry for it and I am glad that he intends next year to stucco this house and to take off the reproach from himself of having 'set the valley of fire'.

This house is magnificently furnished but to my taste much too fine for a country house even putting the idea of comfort out of the question. There is too much Egyptian ornament – Egyptian hieroglyphic figures bronze and gilt but all hideous. In one room called the Egyptian room there is a bed made exactly after the model of Denon's Egyptian bed – a sofa bed broad enough for two alderman embossed gold hieroglyphic *frights* all pointing with their hands distorted backwards at an Osiris or a long armed monster of some sort who sits after their fashion on her hams and heels and hath the likeness of a globe of gold on her lappetted, scaly lappetted head. In another room there is a really curious collection of Raphaels designs of ornaments for the Vatican – from Titus's baths – something like those at Lord Sunderlins. How could Raphaels genius turn to such conceits – for instance branches of trees with groups of singing birds mocking an owl! I should never finish or should make a description fit for an auctioneer if I went through all these rooms. The French furniture is rich and beautiful mahogany veneered more exquisitely and shewing in better taste the veins and knots of the wood than any English workmanship I ever saw but all with clumsy keys as you saw in Paris. In every passage and hall there are collections of frightful monsters in bronze or stone or plaister. One bronze *genius* as I am told he is, about my own height with outstretched long arm offends me most, because I am obliged to come across him ten times a day in passing to my own door. I could with pleasure knock him down and break him in pieces. (Private. The first night I came here the impudent monster kept me a quarter of an hour prisoner in the water closet because I mistook his shadow for the shadow of a real man standing near the door. Do you wonder I owe him a grudge?) There are sundry mechanical impossibilities too in some of the statues which hurt my mechanical feelings for instance a resigned female Cariatides of white stucco whose head in eternal pillory supports a heavy staircase while her feet stand on a globe so small that it could never support her and it seems always slipping from under her – also a slice of a bronze candelabra figure in the dining room with arms painfully holding 12 candle branches heavier and larger than herself and without a resting place for her poor feet – on the contrary with a cruel gold basket hung on her ancles! But most I feel for a classical figure never so used before to my knowledge – The slave taking the thorn out of his foot – a cast in bronze on a pedestal but the pedestal so small that the leg on which the thorny foot is crossed has no support but sticks out in mid air – An eternally painful impossibility that hurts my eyes whenever I go into the dining room. There are some beautiful things however – for instance two casts of Canova's heads of Perseus and Paris and a Psyche of Thorwaldsen's. By the by that Danish stone cutter has jilted the highborn Scotchwoman – the Miss McKenzie who fell in love with him. He found that her fortune was not equal to his expectations and he has set off for Iceland – One way of curing a lady's love. We have had no company here but two or three gentlemen Mr. Harness – agreeable and open hearted – Mr. Moore son of the late Archbishop of Canterbury clever but too much of the Poco curante for me – but not for the fashion – squinting a little and with a mouth that opens crookedly and lips that express scorn but a cela pres very agreeable and high bred and fond of his own comforts as Lambeth could make him! Of Mr. Sharp I need say nothing. You know him and his magic lantern of good things. Some new figures on the slides – Miss Burrowes Mrs. Hopes niece has been the only *femul* we have seen tho Lady Rothes and others called but we escaped from them. Miss Burrowes has been well-*mastered* and has travelled and all that but is an insipid personnage with a flat back and well curled hair. She can *tell* a little about Florence but all her words and movements are so measured that I long to shake her to see if I could shake the affectation out of her and to satisfy myself whether there is or is not any thing else within her. She always moves with her toe pointed down on the carpet and as if she was winning her way between brittle glass or precious china and moving, or standing or sitting she seems evermore as if she had the fear of the five positions before her eyes. But poor thing! as Mrs Candor would say, Who knows but she thinks it her duty and the whole duty of woman? But Mr. Hope really likes her and says that though a spoiled child she is not the least selfish . . .

SUNDAY MORNING . . .

Farewell Mr. Hope calls me to walk. G. Bristow in full feather with a new coat. Mrs. Hogan the housekeeper calls him 'that old gentleman of yours who is always walking about the grounds.' Tell Molly – Love to Kitty – *Hate* to all other inquiring friends . . .

affectionately yours

Maria E

½ after 5 oclock. Just returned from a most beautiful walk with Mr. Hope. I have used the word *Beautiful* in so many different tones of admiration within this last hour that I am afraid I have almost worn it out so I will let it rest as I am instructed to let the Galvanic battery Miss Sebright gave me, rest whenever it is tired that it may recover its power to act.

Pray tell Sophy Ruxton all about Lord Carrington and our intention of going to High Wycombe the 1st of May. She says she is surprised that I do not mention Lord Carrington. Bless her I have not time to mention half the people and things I ought to mention. I could not write to her this moment unless you were to cut me in bits and give me two heads and 2 right hands. When I can only write to one you dearest mother have the first claim of affection duty and gratitude – Lucky and pleasant when all those three go together. I never can thank you enough for lending me Fanny. You shall soon have her back again I hope the better in health and in happiness for her journey. She has just come in from her poney ride and liked it. But here I was interrupted by a dreadful disaster – Mrs. Hope came softly stealing into the little room where we were all three writing and in her hand she held a superb Malachite necklace and cross with gold chains! Oh mother I admired a piece of malachite in a marble table the other day and Mr. Hope explained to me that there is only one mine of it in the world in Russia. And Mrs. Hope has given me this necklace! And I could not refuse her her lips trembled so and she was in such agitation about it.

Fanny is well. She has ridden out every day on a nice little poney with Henry Hope on a ditto and a servant on a prancing chestnut like Wat Tyler. I would not let Mr. Harness, who much desired it, ride with them instead of the servant on said prancing horse because I am told he is a bad rider and I should have been in an agony the whole time beside the real danger. Yesterday we went in the carriage and Fanny rode to see Wotton Mr. Evelyns most beautiful place – Woods worthy of Sylvia indeed! The distance from Deep Dene about four miles. Fanny rode there and back without fatigue. The whole ride delightful through lane and village with every variety of landscape and banks rich and gay (better than rich and rare) with primroses, violets orchises in profusion – White thorns and fruit trees in full blossom – neat cottages and old English country houses of all sizes from noble to simple. The house at Wotton is not pretty but up and down old fashned and interesting from being Wotton with all its traditions. We sent up to ask permission to see the library and an old thin stupid wizzen looking Mr. Evelyn received us with goodnatured awkwardness and told us we were welcome to see whatever we pleased but he knew nothing about his ancestors or their pictures by which he was surrounded. All he could tell us was that there was a portrait of Mr. Evelyn with his book in his hand and he *did* also know a portrait of Tillotson. The library is not nearly so large as Edgeworthstown library nor so pleasant – More like Brianstown – but filled with choice old books all growing damp. The oaf said 'Aye here are more books than I shall ever read Im sure and there are some up there that never were down I dare say since they were put up.' He turned out some old prints before us and old plans 'Since you are curious to see such things.' He was very civil and we were very ungrateful for thinking him insufferably stupid.

Mr. Harness is as far from stupid as possible. I like both Mr. Hs all three *Hs* very much – Hope – Harness and Hitchings. Mr. Harness is one of the most natural characters I ever saw and Mr. Hitchings an excellent clergyman. Both appear the more amiable for liking each other as they do.

I must go out – Mrs Hope waiting. Adieu. We have been very happy here. Tomorrow by tea time at Grove House.

Ever affectionately your scrawler

Maria E

ed. Christina Colvin, *Maria Edgeworth: Letters from England, 1813–1844*, Oxford (1971)

Charlotte Brontë

Born in 1816 in Thornton, Yorkshire, Charlotte Brontë was the eldest daughter of an Irish father, a clergyman named Patrick Brontë, and a Cornish mother. When she was four years of age the family moved to Haworth, also in Yorkshire, where she lived for most of her life, apart from the two years she spent in Brussels as a pupil-teacher. On her return she and her sisters, under the pseudonyms of 'Currer' (Charlotte), 'Ellis' (Emily) and 'Acton' (Anne) Bell, published a collection of poems, which was unsuccessful. She turned to novel-writing and, with *Jane Eyre*, *Shirley* and *Villette*, established her fame. In 1854 she married her father's curate, Mr Nicholls, but died a year later.

FAITH RESTORED

At the age of sixteen Charlotte had completed her formal education, in a school at Roe Head, where she spent eighteen months. Among her particular friends was Ellen Hussey, who was to remain a close friend for many years. In this letter to Ellen, Charlotte records her surprise at receiving a letter from a school friend. It is quite a letter for a girl of sixteen.

JANUARY 13TH, 1832   HAWORTH

Dear Ellen,

The receipt of your letter gave me an agreeable surprise, for, notwithstanding your faithful promises, you must excuse me if I say that I had little confidence in their fulfilment, knowing that when schoolgirls once get home they willingly abandon every recollection which tends to remind them of school, and, indeed, they find such an infinite variety of circumstances to engage their attention, and employ their leisure hours, that they are easily persuaded that they have no *time* to fulfil promises made at school. It gave me great pleasure, however, to find that you and Miss Taylor are exceptions to the general rule. I am sorry to hear that —— has been ill; likewise that Miss Wooler has suffered from bad colds. The cholera still seems slowly advancing, but let us yet hope, knowing that all things are under the guidance of a Merciful Providence. England has hitherto been highly favoured, for the disease has neither raged with the astounding violence, nor extended itself with the frightful rapidity which marks its progress in many of the continental countries. I am glad to hear Mr —— was pleased with Mercy's drawings. Tell her I hope she will derive benefit from the perusal of Cobbett's lucubrations, but I beg she will on no account burden her memory with passages to be repeated for my edification, lest I should not appreciate either her kindness or their merit, since that worthy personage and his principles (whether private or political) are no great favourites of mine.

Remember me to ——, give my love to dear Mary Taylor and little Miss Boisterous, and accept the same, dearest Ellen, from
your affectionate friend,
Charlotte Brontë

HER FATHER'S OPERATION

In this letter of 1846 Charlotte describes to her friend Ellen Hussey her father's eye-operation. She goes on to express her strong opinions on what was probably a very mild flirtation.

Dear Ellen,

The operation is over – it took place yesterday – Mr Wilson performed it, two other surgeons assisted – Mr Wilson says he considers it quite successful but papa cannot yet see anything – The affair lasted precisely a quarter of an hour – it was not the simple operation of couching Mr Carr described but the more complicated one of extracting the cataract – Mr Wilson entirely disapproves of couching.

Papa displayed extraordinary patience and firmness – the surgeons seemed surprised. I was in the room all the time, as it was his wish that I should be there – of course I neither spoke nor moved till the thing was done – and then I felt that the less I said either to papa or the surgeons, the better – papa is now confined to his bed in a dark room and is not to be stirred for four days – he is to speak and to be spoken to as little as possible –

I am greatly obliged to you for your letter and your kind advice which gave me extreme satisfaction because I found I had arranged most things in accordance with it – and as your theory coincides with my practice I feel assured the latter is right – I hope Mr Wilson will soon allow me to dispense with the nurse – she is well enough no doubt but somewhat too obsequious &c. and not I should think to be much trusted – yet I am obliged to trust her in some things –

Your friend Charlotte has had a letter from Mary Taylor – and she was only waiting to hear from one Ellen Nussey that she had received a similar document in order to communicate the fact – if the said Ellen had not got one too – Charlotte would have said nothing about it for fear of inflicting a touch of pain – I have not my letter here or I should send it to you it was written on the voyage – she refers me to 'the long one' for later news – I have not yet seen it.

Greatly was I amused by your accounts of Joe Taylor's flirtations – and yet something saddened also – I think Nature intended him for something better than to fritter away his time in making a set of poor, unoccupied spinsters unhappy – The girls unfortunately are forced to care for him and such as him because while their minds are mostly unemployed, their sensations are all unworn and consequently fresh and keen – and he on the contrary has had his fill of pleasure and can with impunity make a mere pastime of other people's torments. This is an unfair state of things, the match is not equal I only wish I had the power to infuse into the soul of the persecuted a little of the quiet strength of pride – of the supporting consciousness of superiority (for they are superior to him because purer) of the fortifying resolve of firmness to bear the present and wait the end. Could all the virgin population of Birstall and Gomersal receive and retain these sentiments – Joe Taylor would eventually have to vail his crest before them.

Perhaps luckily their feelings are not so acute as one would think and the gentleman's shafts consequently don't wound so deeply as he might desire – I hope it is so.

Give my best love to your Mother and Sisters – Write soon.

C. Brontë

eds T.J. Wise and J.A. Symington, *The Brontës: Their Lives, Friendships and Correspondence in Four Volumes*, University Press, Oxford (1932)

A REPLY TO A POET

This letter is a reply to one from Robert Southey which itself was a reply to one that Charlotte had written him before Christmas, in which she had asked for advice. Southey's reply was kindly, and in it he gently pointed out that if she had known him better beforehand 'you might have had your ardour in some degree abated by seeing a poet in the decline of life, and witnessing the effect which age produces upon our hopes and aspirations'. In fact, Charlotte went on to enjoy a reasonably lengthy correspondence with the poet.

MARCH 16TH, 1837   ROE HEAD

Sir,

I cannot rest till I have answered your letter, even though by addressing you a second time I should appear a little intrusive; but I must thank you for the kind and wise advice you have condescended to give me. I had not ventured to hope for such a reply; so considerate in its tone, so noble in its spirit. I must suppress what I feel, or you will think me foolishly enthusiastic.

At the first perusal of your letter I felt only shame and regret that I had ever ventured to trouble you with my crude rhapsody; I felt a painful heat rise to my face when I thought of the quires of paper I had covered with what once gave me so much delight, but which now was only a source of confusion; but after I had thought a little, and read it again and again, the prospect seemed to clear. You do not forbid me to write; you do not say that what I write is utterly destitute of merit. You only warn me against the folly of neglecting real duties for the sake of imaginative pleasures; of writing for the love of fame; for the selfish excitement of emulation. You kindly allow me write poetry for its own sake, provided I leave undone nothing which I ought to do, in order to pursue that single, absorbing, exquisite gratification. I am afraid, sir, you think me very foolish. I know the first letter I wrote to you was all senseless trash from beginning to end; but I am not altogether the idle, dreaming being it would seem to denote.

My father is a clergyman of limited though competent income, and I am the eldest of his children. He expended quite as much in my education as he could afford in justice to the rest. I thought it therefore my duty, when left school to become a governess. In that capacity I find enough to occupy my thoughts all day long, and my head and hands too, without having a moment's time for one dream of the imagination. In the evenings, I confess, I do think, but I never trouble anyone else with my thoughts. I carefully avoid any appearance of preoccupation and eccentricity, which might lead those I live amongst to suspect the nature of my pursuits. Following my father's advice – who from my childhood has counselled me, just in the wise and friendly tone of your letter – I have endeavoured not only attentively to observe all the duties a woman ought to fulfil, but to feel deeply interested in them. I don't always succeed, for sometimes when I'm teaching or sewing I would rather be reading or writing; but

I try to deny myself; and my father's approbation amply rewarded me for the privation. Once more allow me to thank you with sincere gratitude. I trust I shall never more feel ambitious to see my name in print; if the wish should rise, I'll look at Southey's letter, and suppress it. It is honour enough for me that I have written to him, and received an answer. That letter is consecrated; no one shall ever see it but papa and my brother and sisters. Again I thank you. This incident, I suppose, will be renewed no more; if I live to be an old woman, I shall remember it thirty years hence as a bright dream. The signature which you suspected of being fictitious is my real name.

Again, therefore, I must sign myself

C. Brontë

P.S. – Pray, sir, excuse me for writing to you a second time; I could not help writing, partly to tell you how thankful I am for your kindness, and partly to let you know that your advice shall not be wasted, however sorrowfully and reluctantly it may at first be followed.

C.B.

Muriel Spark (compiler), *The Brontë Letters*, Peter Nevill, London (1954)

Emily Jane Brontë

Emily Brontë was born in Haworth, Yorkshire, in 1818, the second surviving daughter of Patrick Brontë, an Irishman from Co. Down, who had been ordained in the Church of England and obtained a living in Yorkshire. She had contributed to the collection of poetry published by herself and her two sisters, Charlotte and Anne, under the pseudonym of 'Ellis Bell'; despite the relative failure of this publication she has been described as 'one of the most original poets of the century'. Unfortunately her novel, *Wuthering Heights*, published in 1847, did not achieve the esteem it deserved until after her death in 1848.

EMILY'S BIRTHDAY NOTE

Like her younger sister Anne, Emily was not too diligent a correspondent; the two younger girls did, however, share a very close relationship, and instituted an exchange of 'birthday notes' to be opened after a period of four years had elapsed. It may well have been Emily who was the instigator of this rather charming family custom.

A PAPER to be opened
when Anne is
25 years old,
or my next birthday after
if
all be well.
Emily Jane Brontë. July the 30th, 1841.

It is Friday evening, near 9 o'clock – wild rainy weather. I am seated in the dining-room, having just concluded tidying our desk boxes, writing this document. Papa is in the parlour – aunt upstairs in her room. She has been reading *Blackwood's Magazine* to papa. Victoria and Adelaide are ensconced in the peat-house. Keeper is in the kitchen – Hero in his cage. We are all stout and hearty, as I hope is the case with Charlotte, Branwell, and Anne, of whom the first is at John White, Esq., Upperwood House, Rawdon; the second is at Luddenden Foot; and the third is, I believe, at Scarborough, inditing perhaps a paper corresponding to this.

A scheme is at present in agitation for setting us up in a school of our own; as yet nothing is determined, but I hope and trust it may go on and prosper and answer our highest expectations. This day four years I wonder whether we shall still be dragging on in our present condition or established to our hearts' content. Time will show.

I guess that at the time appointed for the opening of this paper we, i.e. Charlotte, Anne, and I, shall be all merrily seated in our own sitting-room in some pleasant and flourishing seminary, having just gathered in for the mid-summer ladyday. Our debts will be paid off, and we shall have cash in hand to a considerable amount. Papa, aunt, and Branwell will either have been or be coming to visit us. It will be a fine warm summer evening, very different from this bleak lookout, and Anne and I will perchance slip out into the garden for a few minutes to peruse our papers. I hope either this or something better will be the case.

The *Gondaland* are at present in a threatening state, but there is no open rupture as yet. All the princes and princess of the Royalty are at the Palace of Instruction. I have a good many books on hand, but I am sorry to say that as usual I make small progress with any. However, I have just made a new regularity paper! and I must *verb sap* to do great things.

> And now I close, sending from far an exhortation of courage,
> courage, to exiled and harassed Anne, wishing she was here.

FOUR YEARS OF FAMILY FORTUNES – AN ALTERNATIVE VIEW

In this birthday note Emily gives her account of the events of the four years since the first exchange of such notes.

THURSDAY, JULY 30TH, 1845   HAWORTH

My birthday – showery, breezy, cool. I am twenty-seven years old to-day. This morning Anne and I opened the papers we wrote four years since, on my twenty-third birthday. This paper we intend, if all be well, to open on my thirtieth – three years hence, in 1848. Since the 1841 paper the following events have taken place. Our school scheme has been abandoned, and instead Charlotte and I went to Brussels on the 8th of February, 1842.

Branwell left his place at Luddenden Foot. C. and I returned from Brussels, November 8th, 1842, in consequence of aunt's death.

Branwell went to Thorp Green as a tutor, where Anne still continued, January, 1843.

Charlotte returned to Brussels the same month, and after staying a year, came back again on New Year's Day 1844.

Anne left her situation at Thorp Green of her own accord, June 1845.

Anne and I went our first long journey by ourselves together, leaving home on the 30th of June, Monday, sleeping at York, returning to Keighley Tuesday evening, sleeping there and walking home on Wednesday morning. Though the weather was broken we enjoyed ourselves very much, except during a few hours at Bradford. And during our excursion we were, Ronald Macalgin, Henry Angora, Juliet Augusteena, Rosabella Esmaldan, Ella and Julian Egremont, Catharine Navarre, and Cordelia Fitapnnold, escaping from the palaces of instruction to join the Royalists who are hard driven at present by the victorious Republicans. The Gondals still flourish bright as ever. I am at present writing a work on the First War. Anne has been writing some articles on this, and a book by Henry Sophona. We intend sticking firm by the rascals as long as they delight us, which I am glad to say they do at present. I should have mentioned that last summer the school scheme was revived in full vigour. We had prospectuses printed, despatched letters to all acquaintances imparting our plans, and did our little all; but it was found no go. Now I don't desire a school at all, and none of us have any great longing for it. We have cash enough for our present wants, with a prospect of accumulation. We are all in decent health, only that papa has a complaint in his eyes, and with the exception of B., who, I hope, will be better and do better hereafter. I am quite contented for myself: not as idle as formerly, altogether as hearty, and having learnt to make the most of the present and long for the future with the fidgetiness that I cannot do all I wish; seldom or ever troubled with nothing to do, and merely desiring that everybody could be as comfortable as myself and as undesponding, and then we should have a very tolerable world of it.

By mistake I find we have opened the paper on the 31st instead of the 30th. Yesterday was much such a day as this, but the morning was divine.

Tabby, who was gone in our last paper, is come back, and has lived with us two years and a half, and is in good health. Martha, who also departed, is here too. We have got Flossy; got and lost Tiger; lost the hawk Hero, which, with the geese, was given away, and is doubtless dead, for when I came back from Brussels I inquired on all hands and could hear nothing of him. Tiger died early last year. Keeper and Flossy are well, also the canary acquired four years since. We are now all at home, and likely to be there some time. Branwell went to Liverpool on Tuesday to stay a week. Tabby has just been teasing me to turn as formerly to 'Pilloputate'. Anne and I should have picked the black currants if it had been fine and sunshiny. I must hurry off now to my turning and ironing. I have plenty of work on hands, and writing, and am altogether full of business.

With best wishes for the whole house till 1848, July 30th, and as much longer as may be, – I conclude.

Emily Brontë

Muriel Spark (compiler), *The Brontë Letters*, Peter Nevill, London (1954)

Anne Brontë

Anne Brontë was born in 1820, in Haworth, Yorkshire, the youngest of the three sisters. She spent several years as a governess and published, as 'Acton Bell', *Agnes Grey*, in 1847, which was based on her experiences. This was followed by *The Tenant of Wildfell Hall*, which portrays a violent drunkard, a character possibly drawn from her brother Branwell. Her eldest sister, Charlotte, describes her as being 'naturally sensitive, reserved and dejected'. She died at Scarborough in 1844.

ANNE'S BIRTHDAY NOTE

Anne was particularly close to her sister Emily who was two years older. The following is one of her reciprocal birthday notes to Emily.

JULY THE 30TH, A.D. 1841   THORP GREEN

This is Emily's birthday. She has now completed her 23rd year, and is, I believe, at home. Charlotte is a governess in the family of Mr. White. Branwell is a clerk in the railroad station at Luddenden Foot, and I am a

111

governess in the family of Mr. Robinson. I dislike the situation and wish to change it for another. I am now at Scarborough. My pupils are gone to bed and I am hastening to finish this before I follow them.

We are thinking of setting up a school of our own, but nothing definite is settled about it yet, and we do not know whether we shall be able to or not. I hope we shall. And I wonder what will be our condition and how or where we shall all be on this day four years hence; at which time, if all be well, I shall be 25 years and 6 months old, Emily will be 27 years old, Branwell 28 years and 1 month, and Charlotte 29 years and a quarter. We are now all separate and not likely to meet again for many a weary week, but we are none of us ill that I know of, and all are doing something for our own livelihood except Emily, who, however, is as busy as any of us, and in reality earns her food and raiment as much as we do.

> How little know we what we are
> How less what we may be!

Four years ago I was at school. Since then I have been a governess at Blake Hall, left it, come to Thorpe Green, and seen the sea and York Minster. Emily has been a teacher at Miss Patchet's school, and left it. Charlotte has left Miss Wooler's, been a governess at Mrs. Sidgwick's, left her, and gone to Mrs. White's. Branwell has given up painting, been a tutor in Cumberland, left it, and became a clerk on the railroad. Tabby has left us. Martha Brown has come in her place. We have got Keeper, got a sweet little cat and lost it, and also got a hawk. Got a wild goose which has flown away, and three tame ones, one of which has been killed. All these diversities, with many others, are things we did not expect or foresee in the July of 1837. What will the next four years bring forth? Providence only knows. But we ourselves have sustained very little alteration since that time. I have the same faults that I had then, only I have more wisdom and experience, and a little more self-possession than I then enjoyed. How will it be when we open this paper and the one Emily has written? I wonder whether the *Gondaland* will still be flourishing, and what will be their condition. I am now engaged in writing the fourth volume of *Solala Vernon's Life*.

For some time I have looked upon 25 as a sort of era in my existence. It may prove a true presentiment, or it may be only a superstitious fancy; the latter seems most likely, but time will show.

Anne Brontë

FOUR YEARS IN THE LIFE OF A FAMILY

In this birthday note we learn of what has happened in the Brontë family since the first such note was penned.

THURSDAY, JULY THE 31ST, 1845

Yesterday was Emily's birthday, and the time when we should have opened our 1841 paper, but by mistake we opened it to-day instead. How many things have happened since it was written – some pleasant, some far otherwise. Yet I was then at Thorp Green, and now I am only just escaped from it. I was wishing to leave it then, and if I had known that I had four years longer to stay how wretched I should have been; but during my stay I have had some very unpleasant and undreamt-of experience of human nature. Others have seen more changes. Charlotte has left Mr. White's and been twice to Brussels, where she stayed each time nearly a year. Emily has been there too, and stayed nearly a year. Branwell has left Luddenden Foot, and been a tutor at Thorp Green, and had much tribulation and ill-health. He was very ill on Thursday, but he went with John Brown to Liverpool, where he now is, I suppose; and we hope he will be better and do better in future. This is a dismal, cloudy wet evening. We have had so far a very cold, wet summer. Charlotte has lately been to Hathersage, in Derbyshire, on a visit of three weeks to Ellen Nussey. She is now sitting sewing in the dining-room. Emily is ironing upstairs. I am sitting in the dining-room in the rocking-chair before the fire with my feet on the fender. Papa is in the parlour. Tabby and Martha are, I think, in the kitchen. Keeper and Flossy are, I do not know where. Little Dick is hopping in his cage. When the last paper was written we were thinking of setting up a school. The scheme has been dropt, and long after taken up again, and dropt again, because we could not get pupils. Charlotte is thinking about getting another situation. She wishes to go to Paris. Will she go? She has let Flossy in, by-the-by, and he is now lying on the sofa. Emily is engaged in writing the Emperor Julius's Life. She has read some of it, and I want very much to hear the rest. She is writing some poetry, too. I wonder what it is about? I have begun the third volume of *Passages in the Life of an Individual*. I wish I had finished it. This afternoon I began to set about making my grey figured silk frock that was dyed at Keighley. What sort of a hand shall I make of it? E. and I have a great deal of work to do. When shall we sensibly diminish it? I want to get a habit of early rising. Shall I succeed? We have not yet finished our *Gondal Chronicles* that we began three years and a half ago. When will they be done? The Gondals are at present in a sad state. The Republicans are uppermost, but the Royalists are not quite overcome. The young sovereigns, with their brothers and sisters, are still at the Palace of Instruction. The Unique Society, about half a year ago, were wrecked on a desert island as they were returning from Gaul. They are still there, but we have not played at them much yet. The Gondals in general are not in first-rate playing condition. Will they improve? I wonder how we shall all be, and where and how situated, on the thirtieth of July, 1848, when, if we are all alive, Emily will be just 30. I shall be in my 29th year, Charlotte in her 33rd and Branwell in his 32nd; and what changes shall we have seen and known; and shall we be much changed ourselves? I hope not, for the worse at least. I, for my part, cannot well be flatter or older in mind than I am now.

Hoping for the best, I conclude.

Anne Brontë

Muriel Spark (compiler), *The Brontë Letters*, Peter Nevill, London (1954)

THE LATE
NINETEENTH
CENTURY

The late nineteenth century saw a great increase in the number of Irish emigrants who wrote letters home to their families and friends; many of these letters have survived, for instance those of Isabella Alice Wyly and Brigid Burke. Far rarer, however, is an example of a letter from home in Ireland to an emigrant, as in the case of Eliza Dalton. Knowledge of events at home was as important to the emigrant as news of their whereabouts and experiences was to friends and relatives at home in Ireland.

Letters of women with literary aspirations and achievements continue, with splendid examples from the pens of Edith Somerville and her collaborator and friend Violet Martin, who together formed the team of Somerville and Ross.

Letters from the relatives of famous men begin to appear, though it is perhaps a matter of contention as to whether Lady Wilde, 'Speranza', was more or less important, or well-known, than her husband. Sir William. Certainly their son, Oscar, went to great lengths to remove any traces of bushel from over his light. His wife, Constance, is certainly less well-known than Oscar – indeed it is quite possible that admirers of Oscar are totally unaware of her existence.

Eliza Dalton

Eliza Dalton was born in 1796 and lived with her husband, a reasonably prosperous farmer, at Athassel Abbey, Co. Tipperary. She died in 1874 at the age of 78.

NEWS FROM IRELAND

This letter from Eliza is unusual in two respects: it is a letter to emigrants, rather than from them, and the emigrants in question were not members of the Dalton family as such, but rather former servants: Ned Hogan and his wife Johana, who had emigrated to New South Wales.

SEPT 4TH 1853   ABBEY

Dear Johana

Need I say I am indebted for the kindness you evinced in writing and also how I rejoice for your welfare. Indeed I should be ungrateful, if I were not interested for you and each of your family. In justice to them I must say that few in humble life better than them left this Country. You wont forget to give them my best wishes, particularly to Mary. I am delighted at the choise she made tell her to pray for me. It has been the will of God to afflict me with a Succession of Severe trials, nor am I rid of them yet. Mr Denis is in the last Stage of Consumption. Very probable before this reaches you He will be laid in his resting place. He has the Sympathy of all who know him but what avails it to those who are conscious of immediate danger. You will also be sorry to hear that your kind friend the Rev Michael Mc.Donnel caught fever in discharge of his duty Survived only a few days. He was waked and buried in the Chapel of Cashel, amidst the wailings of the poor, for whom he Seemed to live. He was only a few months Curate to his Uncle and lest he may die in debt had his life insured for £100. His poor Sister the Nun daily visits his Grave not to weep but pray. You Cant expect much news from me whose thoughts & attention are engaged by my dying son. Mr John is at home Since last April you never saw him looking better. He does not like the climate of America. Mr Willy was well when last I heard from him. Father Matthew met him and Said he is a credit to his Country.

I sent your letter to your Aunt McGlin knowing it would be a comfort to her and enclose you her note. Since last November we have not heard from Matt Blake his address Robert Cassels Esqr. Islend Lake Cooma Manaroo. Will you give them my best wishes. You can also say that two of James Ryans Sisters left Abbey for Melbourn last June. James Magrath, the Coopers daughter is also in Melbourn. Julia Kenedy left for America her Sister has an exellent situation in England. The Turners who lived with Mr Wayland are in your old habitation. Mr Wayland gone to Austrilia his family in Dublin. The police are removed from Mough. Ned Kenedy Steward there as usual he will miss them. Why Should you Speak of triffling postage to me who Shall always be anxious to hear from you, and also expect that nothing will prevent your writting. Mrs. Quinlan was here last Sunday we were talking a long time of you. Her Son will be ordained next Summer. Mart [*Margaret*] Dwyers best wishes to you all. She is sorry that those of her family who went to America Are not in your Country.

Adieu dear Johana

And Blieve me

Most Sincerely Yours

Eliza Dalton

David Fitzpatrick, *Oceans of Consolation: Personal Accounts of Irish Migration to Australia*, University Press, Cork (1994)

Isabella Alice Wyly

Isabella Wyly was born in 1833 and at the age of eighteen she emigrated to Australia, arriving in Port Adelaide in 1851. She was shortly joined by her uncle Alexander Wyly, with his wife Elizabeth and their five children.

SEVEN YEARS LATER

In this letter Isabella writes to Matilda Wyly, her brother's widow, who had taken over her mother's drapery shop in Newry, Co. Down. It clearly took Isabella a long time to attempt to console her widowed sister-in-law.

JULY 2TH 1856   ADELAIDE

My dearest Matilda

After the Silence and separation of seven long years, I at last take the opperturnity of writing to you, for I feel very ancious to here from you & your dear little ones. It was a very painful shock to me, and all of us, to here of your severe trial. May the lord support you under all. He will be the Father to the Fatherless and the friend of the Widows. Can it be posable that He is gone. I can carsly believe it sometimes, but I am afraid it is to true. My onely hope and trust is that He has made a Change for the better, and may we all meet where separation shall be no more.

Aunt Elizabeth received a letter from her Father which told us. It was a great blow to us knowing the misrable[?] way which he was living in before we left home, but I hope and trust he had reformed air long he went to his long home.

Dear Matilda who should hav thought the many changes that would take Place in so short a time, in the Wyly family as there has.

I suppose you hav herd before this of dear Aunt Fanny & Uncle Roberts death. The were but 3 Months in Melburne when dear Aunt Fanny died and dear little Charly & the little Baby which was only 3 weeks old, were all laid in the one tomb, and a very short time after their Uncle Robert came to Adelaide, to see us and to make arrangements to come and settle alto[ge]ther in Adelaide, and returned to Melbourne agen to settle things there, but it pleased the lord to remove Him also, so the dear Children were left to do for themselfs. Tomas and Alexander were with Aunt Elizabath for a long time, but Alax has got a Situation in a drapers Shop now and Tom remains sill with Aunt. Henry is sill in Melburn in a good Situation. Ruth is Marryed, and has got a dear little Girl. She is very happy and has made a very comfortable home.

What changes, and I suppose there has been just as many at home. It does not seem home to me now, all seems to hav gone either to their long home, or to others Parts of the world. We hav herd of the death of dear old Grand Papa and Grand Mama, also of Uncle Charles Miridith. What a change for Poor Aunt Lucy, to be nocked out of a comfortable home.

Uncle Alaxander and family thak God has been blest with helth and strength since the hav been in Austrilia, altho the have not been so Prospers as many that come here and the hav had a great difficulty to get on with his large family, for every thing is so much more expensive here that it is atome so the hav had a grand struggle to get on but I hope the will see better days. Aunt Elizabeth has been blest with a dear little son, which is now just 6 months old. He is a beautiful Boy and the Pet of the home so the hav great reson to be thankful when the look at the affliction of other branches of the family. Robert is getting quite a young Man, in his 17 year, and in a drapers Shop getting on nicely. Fanny & Hinriata & Willy ar all going to Chool, Alexander Peel is getting a great big Boy.

I suppose I should not know dear Edward, or little Susan. I should so like to see them. I expect the quite forget the ever had an Aunt Isabella by this time, but I never shall forget them. Perhaps you think it is out site out of mind with me but it is not the case, for you all ar many times my evening thoughts, for that is my only time, for thinking.

I hav told you litle of my own history as yet. I hav great reson to be thankful in fact I have no reson to regret my coming to Austrilia, for I am much better of than I ever should for been atome. On my first arivel to

Adelaide, I felt a stranger in a strange Land, which is now 5 years since I left home. I new no one, nor had I a friend to take my hand, but thank God I had Him who Never has forsakeing. He be my Father & Friend and I trust he ever will be if we look to Him.

A short time after my arivel I met a friend in Mrs. Capten Bagget which is well know in West Meath. I had letters for her from Ireland. She received me very kindly and obtained a Situation in a drapers Shop. You know I new nothing about the buisnes, but with an effort and a kind Master I got on, and was receiveing 10s/ Per week. In a short time after, I received 12s/ and then 15s/ week and now I am in Posecion of £52 Per Ann. So you may think that was encourageing for a young biginer. You will say, it a great change for me for the better, and I never felt more happy in my life than I do now that I am independent of everyone. There is no bread sweeter th the bread you work for yourself. I should hav been a long time in poor old Dublin before I should show so well as I hav done here. I am very comfortable and happy, and hav great reson to be thankful.

I hope Mrs. Bell is quite well. Please give my kind love to her. I soppose you are stoping in Newry now. Tell me all about it when you write for I am very ancious to here. I often wish you were with us in Adelaide. Aunt & Uncle, seems so lonely, for want of some of her deer friends to be neer me and console her. She does not seem to feel it so much now as she used when she first came to Australia for she is getting used to it now, and getting reconsiled to it. It is sutch a change from home where she could have You, or Aunt Lucy or some friend to come and see her, but here she has but Me, and that is but once a Week. But we must be satisfied now we ar here, for I soppose it was our lot or we should not have come.

I soppose you have herd of the Gold fields. It drove many from the comfortable homes some for the better as others for the worse. Uncle Alaxander went but did not suckseed in getting a fortion as many thought the would. He got very bad helth and would not stop to give it a very fair trial, for it was a missrable Place to be sure. A great many came from Ireland on heering the news of Gold fields, but nowon we new but Mr. O

Gorman arived in Melburne. We have not seen him yet. I should think Ireland was nearly cleared of the Poor People, for there has been so many Emigrants Ships arived here Miserable Irash. I expect it is very much improved for the better. Oh I should like to see, dear old Ireland once more before I die. I hope I shall.

Ruth and Mrs Shadget which is her name now intends going home shortly, but I soppose that will be to England, for he is Engelish. She is very much altered for the better, and is quite a little Mother. Sutch changes. She has had trial enough since she left home. She had noone but herself, when her deer Mama & Brother died and was left the deer little Baby which lived b 3 weeks with her. It was a great mersie it was taken. Aunt Elizabath felt it very much that the were not with her, that she could renderd her a little comfort in her truble but unfortionately the arived in Melburne. Henry has never come to Adelaide yet so we have not seen him since his arival, but he is doing very well.

Dear Matilda, I seem to have sutch a deal to tell you and questions to ask you I am afraid I shoul try your Pations to read it, but I hope our silence will not be so long agen. You do not know how delight we shall all be to heer from you. I shall be ancisly looking out for the next Mail. We have one every Month, so we have every opportunity.

I will send you an Adelaide Paper. Please sen me an Irash one for it is a treat to see the news, we get one so seldom.

I hav had a great wish to get dear little Susans and Ewards liknesses. Tell me if you could hav an oppurtunity to get them for me. I should dearly like to have them. I hope and trust the will be a comfort to you now, which I expect the ar, and me He who will be the Father to the Orphans, keep them in the wright Path, which leads to Joys Above and where all dear friends meets to sepperate no more. Oh that day was come. It would be a happy meeting, woul it not.

Bein limited to time, as the Mail starts tomorrow, I must bring this scribble to a conclusion, leeving you and your deer little ones to the care of Him who will never forsake, tho all friends may. He will never if we do not forsake Him, and if it should Please Him that we should not meet agen in this World may we all meet in the next where all truble shall be at an end, around the throne of God in Heaven, there to reign with Him forever. That is the enerest and sincer Prayer of

Yours ever fond and Affectionate Sister
Isabella Wyly

Joyned by all friends in Kindest love to you and yours &
Mrs. Bell, except the Same from
Isabella Wyly

Direct your letter to
North Adelaide
South Austrilia.
I enclose my place of residence. Excuse all, in haste.

David Fitzpatrick, *Oceans of Consolation: Personal Accounts of Irish Migration to Australia*, University Press, Cork (1994)

Lady Jane Francesca Wilde (née Elgee) ('Speranza')

Jane Elgee was born in Wexford in 1826. As 'Speranza' she contributed to *The Nation* and when Charles Gavan Duffy was in prison she replaced him as leader-writer. In 1848 she issued a call to arms on behalf of the Young Irelanders and proclaimed her authorship at Duffy's trial, but was not prosecuted. In 1851 she married William Wilde, an eye and ear surgeon. In 1854, an eventful year, she gave birth to her second son, Oscar Fingal O'Flahertie Wills Wilde; her husband received a knighthood and she was taken to court for libel by Mary Travers, a patient of her husband's with whom he had had an affair. After her husband's death in 1876 she moved to London and died, in somewhat straitened circumstances, in 1896, during Oscar's imprisonment.

A MOST UNFORTUNATE LETTER

Lady Wilde had become increasingly distressed and angry at the
behaviour of Mary Travers, who had launched a programme of
provocation against the Wilde family, herself in particular. Lady Wilde
wrote to Mary's father, a Dr Travers – a letter which Mary subsequently
found while rummaging through her father's papers. She promptly took it
to a solicitor and a writ for libel was issued to Lady Wilde and her
husband, Sir William. When the case was heard the court found in favour
of Mary Travers but awarded her one farthing in damages. This is the
letter responsible.

MAY 6   FROM LADY WILDE TO DOCTOR TRAVERS, TOWER, BRAY

Sir

You may not be aware of the disreputable conduct of your daughter at
Bray, where she consorts with all the newspaper boys in the place,
employing them to disseminate offensive placards in which my name is
given, and also tracts in which she makes it appear that she has had an
intrigue with Sir William Wilde. If she chooses to disgrace herself, that is
not my affair; but as her object in insulting me is the hope of extorting
money, for which she has several times applied to Sir William Wilde, with
threats of more annoyance if not given, I think it is right to tell you that
no threat or additional insult shall ever extort money for her from our
hands. The wages of disgrace she has so largely treated for and demanded
shall never be given to her.

Jane Wilde

POST-TRIAL INDIGNATION

Lady Wilde had a Swedish friend, Mme Rosalie Olivecrona, with
whom she maintained a fairly regular correspondence. In the
aftermath of the trial she wrote this letter to her which displays her
feelings well.

JANUARY 1, 1865

My dear Madame Olivecrona,

You know of course by this of the disagreeable Law affair in which we have been involved. I send you a few extracts from the various papers. Please ask Professor Olivecrona to show them to Baron Dübben and Magnus Ritzens.

The simple solution to the affair is this – This Miss Travers is mad – all the family are mad too –. She was very destitute and haunted our house to borrow money and we were very kind to her as we pitied her – but suddenly she took a dislike to me amounting to hatred – and the endeavour to ruin my peace of mind assumed a series of anonymous attacks. Then she issued vile publications in the name of *Speranza*, accusing my husband. I wrote to her father about them, and she took an action for libel against me. It was very annoying, but of course no one believed her story. All Dublin has called on us to offer their sympathy, and all the medical Profession here and in London have sent letters expressing their entire disbelief of the (in fact) impossible charge. Sir Wm. will not be injured by it, and the best proof is that his professional hours never were so occupied as now. We were more anxious about our dear foreign friends who could only hear through the English papers which are generally very sneering on Irish matters. But happily all is over now and our enemy has been signally defeated in her efforts to injure us.

I have a book of poems out. I shall try to send them to you. Thanks for two magazines, but your translation of 'The Exodus' has not arrived yet. Pray tell our dear friends the Broems all about our late troubles, and the cause of them. I hope you will write to me soon and say where Lotten is now. Give our best love to her.

And with affectionate regards.

THE INDIGNATION CONTINUES

'The Exodus' was a poem Lady Wilde had written about Irish emigration. Rosalie had translated it into Swedish and sent this to her friend with comfort and reassurance. In her reply Lady Wilde thanks her and keeps her up to date with the Travers saga.

MARCH 23, 1865

My dear Friend,

I have received at last quite safely your really *beautiful* and vigorous translation of my poem. Some of the Swedish words are so musical, as for instance '*forbönad*' and I was complimented I feel by the remarks presenting it, including *me* amongst such eminent names. If I could but read Swedish well! but even what I did know is fading away from want of practice. When you come over next, bring over some Swedes to *live here*, or if some nice young girl intending to be a governess wished to reside in an English family for an opportunity to learn *English* I would like to have her – not to pay her – but as a visitor and she could practise French and German speaking with our German governess. This is one of my dreams for learning Swedish. I wonder will it be accomplished. Your kind note was most welcome. I know all your numerous engagements so I never *expect* you to answer me, and I am *grateful* when you do. With regard to that extraordinary woman Miss Travers. She is certainly mad. She has now taken an action for Libel against a newspaper here because of articles showing up her mad and absurd statements. There is madness in her family. Her brother was in a Lunatic Asylum. We were so kind to her always because she was a doctor's daughter, and was very poor, and we tried to get her literary employment as she had *some* ability, and she hated me exactly because I was so kind to her, and nothing made her so jealous as my *literary* reputation. But all this brooded *silently* in her mind. It was not until I had given up her acquaintance on account of her madness that she poured forth her hoarded malignity. However as regards *us* her wicked designs have entirely failed.

I do hope you and the professor will come over again. Your brother will tempt you. I shall send a copy of my poems to you *by post* if I can, and one to Lotten. They have sold greatly in Ireland, but are not suited to *English* taste you may suppose. Oh what an incubus this English Government is on our country. It strangles all life. What a charming intellectual life you all live at Upsala, and Lotten is writing a *novel* I hear. There could be some grand historical novels founded on Swedish history.

Terence de Vere White, *The Parents of Oscar Wilde: Sir William and Lady Wilde*, Hodder and Stoughton, London (1967)

Brigid (Biddy) Burke

Brigid was born in Balrobuck Beg, Co. Galway, in 1859, where her parents occupied a reasonable-sized farm, in an area which was still largely Irish-speaking. She emigrated to Australia in 1880 with her brother Patrick.

DRINK MY HEALTH

In this letter to her father and mother Biddy, after asking all the standard questions about her family at home, tells them something about the strange country she is in. It is interesting that permanent recollections of stories of the Famine still haunt her, nearly forty years later.

MAY THE 5: 1884   BRISBANE

My Dearest father & mother

I for once in 12 months sit to have a few words of conversation with you by a message which I must say is my hardest Job to get through. I got Your letter about 10 days ago which I often wanderd ware You dead or what became of You. As for my Brother & sisters I Quite forgive them as they have got children of their owne to & me a child or a lost lam far away from home & nation. To think my father & mother at the end of a long year could cast a thout on me & wright me a letter. Wasent it a chearing present to a true hart from the Dearest frind.

Well now I must thank god for his kindness to spare you they health to do so & also for my own health which I am enjoying grand. I would like to know what did do to my Brother Jack & Winney. One of those fine days I shall encourage some of those girls away from them as I intend to live an old maid. John I heare they ar growing up fine girls like their Aunt Biddy as Mary A used to say when she used to call me they Black Top & denie her father & mother & tell her mother Winney to go home to Clude & take Dinea & leave Vronkey with her. Dont I often wish I could see them now & that strange girl Keattey. I hope she is lik her ant Biddy as well.

I suppose my Sister Mary hasent got a Bit of paper to soil on a sister. I shanent write again untill I write to my boy Martin. I am glad to here what a fine stout woman Mary became & also I am sorrow for her sister in law Mrs Sulvan of Galway for they wreched life her Mother in law is given her. I here she abuses her fine. I hope M. Walsh is well & as for his sones I supose they ar fine men now. I am comming home one of those days to have a look & a fine old talk to they lot of Yea & father. You never told anny thing about my uncle Larrance what became of him & family. I supose M.A. is a grown up woman & Mick a big man now. Also my uncle Ml how ever is he. I supose Bridget & Henery ar grown up as well also Young William. I dare day I would see a change their now & not forgeting Dear old Mrs Goley which I must call her. How is she & has she got onely one boy & the Dear little soul I expect she has onely 2 girls. How ar they all & not forgetting Aunt Biddy or Aunt Peg also all my cousins & friends & not forgeting the old neighbours of sweet Balrobuck beg. I suppose it as green & as wet as ever.

I am glad that stock is standing a good price but I am sorrow for the corn & & things to get to such a loe price. I supose the potatoes ar still getting Black. Theire is no such a thing as a black potae in Queensland & they native potates we can plant the stalks like gerreamen slips at home in pots. They plant them the same here in the fields & potatoes grows as large as turnips at home. These ar Called sweet potatoes. We have the English potates the same as the home potatoes & turnips & all sorte of vegetables the same as home & anny amount of Beef & mutton & also of meat. Beef is 3½ a lb mutton the same veal & pork from 4d to 6 pence a pound tea 1s. 10d a pound sugar 3 a lb. potatoes ar 1s. a stone to 1s. 6 flour 1½d a pound fowles 5s a pair geese 14s a pair turkeys pound to 25s a pair & every thing is much dear this year than ever fore the summer been so hot.

It was the hotest summer in Queensland with the last 20 years. You must think it was hot when the plaits on the dresser should be handled with a cloth. I dont think we had a wet day with the last 12 mounths. We might have a storm or 3 since but not a wet day. Altogether they men cannot sit Idle in this country from wet weather. Now the summer is over

& the winter comming on I am so glad. I did feel the heat so much boath night & day we could not sleep. It was Quite enough for us to keep the the sweet of our facess.

I suppose Yea had a cold winter of it home & I dare say father & Mother you had a lonely Christmas of it, & so had I. My brother Patt is out the Bush with the last 14 Mounths. I expected him in at Christmas time & his job was not finished & did not come. He is comming into town in 3 mounth time but I here from everry week. Dont think for a moment its for anny gammling he is in the Bush. No he is a good boy & works 10 hours a day for 12s & is saving a lot of money. There are young fellows in this town with they last 10 years & they ar not worth a penney & that is not like poor Patt. He works hard for it & knows how to save it. A lot of Camps in the Bush in tents & feels as happy as the day is long & each man takes it in turn a week cooking & dont they have nice tea.

Now I must tell you some about my uncle. He came to pay me a visit about 2 mounths ago. He feel alright & also all they family. He was saying something about gone home in a year or 2 if he would be spared. I might goe that is if Patt comes well all goe & see the old sod once more. But I dont supose I could live there now altho its the deepest thought in my heart does the water still come into the Yard in winter times & I supose all the Visstoers they same as ever. Dont I often think of them times.

Well now about my owne self I am in grand health & is enjoying Queensland verry much. I am sorrow that I hadent come 5 years before I did come I would have a lot of money now. That is when my mother used call me a foulish girl & now every body tell me I have got too much sence but it dosent matter. When I grow older & save some more money I can live Quite happy then. I am sending you one three pounds for to drink my health & once more. Well now my Dearest father & Mother I hope you are well & also My Dear old Brother John & Winney. I am making none difference nor never will for I know that Winney will be as kind to You father & Mother as if she was a daughter of Your owne.

And does my poor Mother get as bad a head ache as ever. My head gets verry bad sometimes eather they heat or the cold does not agree with it. I have to nearly always keep a hat one in the house & its makes me often think of my poor Mothers head. They Doctors say its from the cold in the feet. I wore cloth boots & I got a wetting from Getting cought in thunder Storm & got my feet wett & a dreadfull bad cold in the head & eever since then my head is tender but now I am carefull. Thunder storms is verry dangese in this countrey they come in less than a minnits notice. So Mind You Mother be sure & keep warm boots one & the Feaver is verry bad in this climat & there is a lot of people dinen. Some days ther is from 2 to 3 deaths in the Hospital thoes that has no home to go to & a lot more from they homes as well. If you neglect Yourself in this country Your as soon Done for.

Now I Must talk to the Girls which I am glad to here that they filling up My old home. Try & bring them up well John & dond keep them at home from School & Winny mind & give a Mothers advise to each of them for you know that it takes a girl all her time to keep her place. I often think of My Mother now how she used to talk to me. This is the place that foolish girls ar knowing. & dont forget to get them boots. Well now I suppose you will be tirde of reading my letter.

I must conclud with fond Love & remaining your daughter & a
loving sister & a sincere Aunt untill Death.

B. Burke.

David Fitzpatrick, *Oceans of Consolation: Personal Accounts of Irish Migration to Australia*, University Press, Cork (1994)

Edith Oenone Somerville

Edith Somerville was born on the island of Corfu in 1858, where her father's regiment was stationed, but grew up at Drishane House, the family home in Castletonshend, Co. Cork. She developed an interest in art and in 1886, while working on a commission to illustrate three serials, first met her cousin Violet Martin, with whom she formed the literary partnership of Somerville and Ross (her cousin having taken on the pseudonym 'Martin Ross'). Together they published three volumes of the famous 'Irish RM' series, beginning in 1889 with *Some Experiences of an Irish RM*. After Violet Martin's death in 1915 she continued writing in their joint name until her own death in 1949.

AMATEUR THEATRICALS

In this letter to Violet, Edith describes a charity theatrical performance in the town hall in Skibbereen, in which Violet's brother, Robert, was involved. From the 'dictionary' of family words compiled by Violet and Edith, we know that 'flahoola' – a word of Irish origin – describes a large loud woman of stupendous vulgarity while 'minauderings', from the French minauder, *'to mince', describes the transparent devices of hussies.*

SEPTEMBER 5TH 89   DRISHANE
BED 1.15 A.M.

My dear Martin

At this unearthly hour I will say a few words to you. The second night of the play is over, and the whole show is done. It has been very successful. The first night was the very biggest house I have ever seen in Skib. That big town hall *packed*. We took between £27 and £30 – but don't know for certain – all the country was there. 112 three shilling seats alone! Egerton and Robert had worked like blacks with the most invaluable help from Percy's servant and a coast guard, and you cant think what a pretty stage they made. I was perfectly amazed – it really was as nice as possible. You must get Robert to describe it to you. In 'Uncle's Will', Ethel wore that pretty blue and red tea gown, with plenty of old paste and her own hair. She looked awfully nice, as the rouge and the blackening of the eyes were very becoming; and I think – privately and confidentially – that, taken all round, she acted the best of the whole lot. Robert was certainly good, but Ethel really *was* the part. In 'Uncle's Will' Egerton was really poor; dull and heavy, and rather feeling for his words all the time, which made the prompting very nervous work, but in 'Pillycoddy' though not word perfect, he acted enchantingly, and was extremely funny, and his makeup was perfect. A photograph is going to be done of us all so you will see what it was like. As Mrs. Pillycoddy, Ethel wore a huge fair wig – (what Robert *would* call a 'Totty wig') – my black sailor hat and a white dress, with a huge pink sash. H. had an immense red wig, a white bonnet with pink roses, a pink striped skirt, red silk body and my covert coat – She came on in Ethel's red coat, and carried a huge carpet bag and the giantess's parasol. She had a very amusing song to the tune of the 'Pilgrim of Love' in which she had to wave and brandish the carpet bag and umbrella, after the manner of grand opera, and she did it *capitally*. You wouldn't have believed how well she did it; and the red wig gave her a terrific vulgar flahoola prettiness that fetched the audience and her whole scene with Ethel went very well. Poor Robert's young man's wig as 'Charles' was awful dull brown mop-head. By dint of cutting it was made to look decent, but I must say it was a relief to see his bald pate again. The painting however gave him also a vulgar stagey good looks which went down with the people, and he is such a favourite in Skib that he could do whatever he liked. His acting was excellent – quiet and confident – and you know that he 'never would get stuck for a word,' and no matter how much he gagged he always got back to his cue right. You never heard anything like the encores for his songs in the concert. There was a perfect storm – Mrs. Morrogh sang 'You sang to me' and 'For you' as encore. Mrs H. Brougham sang very indifferently. Dully, and without any sympathy and no great display of voice. We vamped up an encore for her, and then found that her encore song had been left behind! She wouldn't sing the last verse of her song, (a second rate English song) again, so finally retired, I was sorry for the poor creature; it was very awkward, but if she was more amiable and less conceited about her singing, I would have had more pity for her. I was less nervous than you might have thought. I find that a curious kind of philosophical courage comes to me with the occasion, and I managed to worry along, and sang my song without any mishap. I cant act, but I can contrive a sort of imitation of acting that is good enough for a fifth rate audience. Robert sang the 'Blatherumskite' and I sang the chorus with him and we danced round together, which fetched the crowd satisfactorily. 'Pillycoddy' went awfully well tonight, far better than yesterday, which was a pity, as there was only a very small house, about two hundred at the outside. I was nearly broken down by laughing once – Robert and I were fooling. He pretends to forget the name of my master and says 'Pilli – Pilly?' so I said '*Coddy*' (which was gag) with minauderings, thereon Robert in the fattest of brogues said 'Caady is it? Well go and tell Caady etc.' which was also gag, and sounded so like Conny, said with a cold in the head, that I began to bellow with laughter. Moreover he looked the image of an appalling male Katie. It luckily was all right that I should laugh, but anyhow I couldn't have helped it. He had a reddish yellow scratch wig and a red beard, and he looked *too* like Katie after she has been washing her hair. I think you would have died of him. We have had a wearing day. Mrs Morrogh came at twelve. Captain Ridley, Mr. Clark (good-looking and pleasant) and Mr. Hibbert (rather unwholesome but a pleasant youth and a stout) all came at two and the moment afterwards in came Sissy Cholmondeley and Dick and Carrie Webb – having come from Derry on the chance of finding us in. Finally after lunch four from the Rectory. It was deeply provoking as I could see nothing of Sissy. It has struck two, and I am writing so dull and putrid a letter that I must stop and try to go to sleep – Goodnight – I *wish* you were here. Bed.

8.30 a.m. – Thursday. – I resume. The Chimp* did band. V. was to have done it, but she was so badly wanted to prompt, and played so uncertainly from nervousness, that we ran the Chimp in, to his intense disgust, but he was a tower of strength and imparted a moral courage such as – for me – only he and Hildegarde inspire. She accompanied R in his songs and did it splendidly. I shall see him today, and will ask him what he shall sing at Oughterard. 'Ballyhooley' and 'Killaloe' and

---

* Chimp: Cameron, eldest brother of E.E.S.

'Enniscorthy' and 'O'Hara' were what he gave on the two nights here – I never saw any human being who took the stage as well as he does. It really is delightful to feel the atmosphere of affectionate swagger that he sheds upon the audience. (Don't tell him this) and he just got every last point out of those songs, they were as dry as lemons when he had done with them. You may well say that we shall be wrecks by the end of this week. Tonight we have a dinner for the Ronnies and tomorrow we have an 'impromptu dance' and we shall have to *clear out the drawing room for it*. Jack is to take the men out shooting, so that they will be out from under our feet. I am faintly bored at this prospect. If only the dance were to be somewhere else it would be so far preferable but 'Belial' Adams has no idea of getting one up for some time, and when she does there will be no one to dance with as these soldiers go off next Thursday. Cameron and Captain Ridley are deeply gratifying about the Shocker and have evidently read it with the greatest attention, and discussed the characters with much discrimination. I do think that the people in it are real people. Uncle Jos told mother that he thought it was extremely well written but that it bored him almost to tears from want of interest, though volume two improved a little. It certainly does go a bit slower than the run – you might say the rush – of his penny dreadfuls and French abominations. Old Grunnums said she had sat up till 11.30 to finish it and was very complimentary. She specially noticed the excellence of the brogue, and commended 'Ferretting'. She has written to Melbourne for it, besides many other places. All here, Mother and Ethel included, say they notice no bad words, except O'Neill's Devil in the ball chapter re Mimi – and we will *not* cut them out of Slide 42. You know Aunt Gig knows a friend (or cousin) of Bentley's; this woman said that Bentley had taken the Herring to a seaside place (appropriate) to read, and told her that it was very clever. This is the best criticism we have had yet, as it means he would look kindly on future work. If we ever get the chance of writing together again. I am longing to see the *Sunday Times*. R was speaking of him the other day and he was an extremely clever fellow who hadn't yet got his chance. It is 9.15. I ought to get up, but I know breakfast will be very late, and it is a wet day –

and I don't want to have any more of it than I can help. What we are to do with these awful men heaven only knows. I trust you didn't go to that dance; it wouldn't have been good enough. I hope Potter will send you the wrong '*Eagles*'.* I never knew anyone so forward and pleni-tudinous as you – Never . . .

Lunch time. The whole morning has been spent in prating to the Chimp and his three men . . . They are all free 'nice things' pleasant and ready to be pleased, but it weeries me to have to play up, but I know the Chimp expects it. There is lunch – and here is post and no time to do more than end up – I am not sorry about the saddle – I expect it would never have fitted Sorcerer. But all the same Day is a fool. Don't expect to hear from me for some time – too harassed.

Yours

Edith

Love to 'the dear old Sod'**

The Death of her Mother

In this letter to Violet, Edith describes, with great sensitivity, her feelings at the death of her mother and muses on the whole business of dying.

FRIDAY NIGHT

Dear Martin

I can't go to sleep, I have tried but it is no use, so I have lighted my candle and will try to think that I am talking to you. Your letter came this morning, and the flowers came just in time. They came by train, with very many others; Cameron opened them and put them in the

---

* The Skibbereen *Eagle*, local newspaper.
** Martin's mama. A reference to the introduction of Robert Martin at a concert as 'a son of the Dear Old Sod'.

carriage that was full of flowers, then he came up to my room, where I was sitting with Hildegarde and Papa, and told me that they had come and gave me the note. I made him bring them up to me. It was late, but I could not let them go without seeing them. They were most beautiful and as fresh as if they had only just been gathered. I could not do as you asked me. I had only time to look at them and let Cameron hurry down with them, but I wrote the card as if it were to go on them. I don't know where to begin. It all feels like one continuous dream of pain that began on Tuesday morning. I don't know when it is going to end. I know you will tell me it is morbid and foolish but most of the things that come back to me are of words and actions that I was sorry for even at the time and now. – And then I feel as if I have never been a bit demonstrative to her or ever let her know how I felt – except indeed when I was angry or provoked. I know she took pleasure out of us all, but I feel now as if I might so easily have done so much more. That there were so many times ('like golden coins squandered, and still to pay') when I was snubbing or beastly – I dont say all of this for you to contradict me – but because I must get it out of my heart. I dont think I have told you anything. On Monday the doctor said her progress was perfectly satisfactory. On the afternoon she told us she felt she had turned the corner – (Yes I did tell you.) How could you ask me to run away down to the Cottage and let Aylmer bear all the brunt alone? It wasn't like you, and I can't think you wished me to do it. For one thing I should have gone mad there. It has been, up here, incessant arrangements and giving of orders and seeing that things were done and that H. didn't do them. Her pluck was quite splendid, but yesterday afternoon she broke down, (in health I mean) and Egerton and I drove her into bed in my room. Hadden was here – we had sent for him to *order* Papa not to go to the funeral; he said she was all right, but must keep quiet in bed and be spared strong emotion. I thanked God that I had persuaded her not to go in and see mother. She is much better this evening and has been in bed all day, a good thing, as we managed to keep Papa down here with her, and he was spared all the sights or rather *sounds*. He never knew when they took the coffin up last night or brought it down this morning – I went in on Wednesday to see her. She looked most beautiful, but so terribly, utterly, remote. I could not feel that it was she. It was a beautiful mask that her soul had worn, and now that it had been cast aside it had taken on a cold sort of serenity, a character of its own, quite apart from hers. In a curious way, seeing what had been her, reconciled me to leaving her alone in the cold half dark silent room. I felt that she was not there. I thought of her meeting Aunt Florry, and telling Minnie what a success the *Real Charlotte* had been and how, for her part, she had much preferred the Mad Dog Paris story. Aylmer and Emmie weren't with me. It is no use to try and tell you what they and Egerton and H. have been. Whenever A. gave himself time to think you could see how shattered he was by grief, but his pluck was beyond what I could possibly have believed. Boyle could not have been stronger or more reliable. As for Egerton I need not tell you of him. He has been everything – so helpful and tender and absolutely unselfish – and his and Aylmer's care for Papa was quite beautiful (it sounds trite but I can think of no other word.) On the night she died they sat up with him and sank all their own grief in trying to calm and comfort him. I could not cry that night – my heart felt like a hot stone and my mind was beating against the incredible truth, like the sea against those awful Arran cliffs. Emmie and H. and I all huddled together in E's room and the house was all alight and people going to and fro in the passages. We had got down a second nurse that day from Cork, a very nice woman too, and they did all that was necessary. I can remember that when at about half past eleven, we were taken in to see her for the last time, the two nurses were standing with tears running down their faces, one on each side of the bed, and I can see that young Doctor O'Mara's pitiful face as he held her pulse. I can't believe it now. I can see her stumping up from Glen B. to lunch, with her eyes on the ground, planning – 'I'm an awful planner' she always used to say – or pinning us with her eyes as we told her of Mildred's latest enormity. I tell myself that she may have been taken away from possible calamity, and that for her it may be best, and all the rest of it, but when I think of her innocent joie de vivre and her unconquerable gaiety I find it a cruel fate that did not let her have a little more of this world that she was happy in. Poor Cameron only arrived by the early mail this morning. Everything was against him, the mail boat three hours late, etc. Luckily A.E, Emmie and I woke early and we had drugged H. and Papa with sulphonal so they did not stir. He was quite broken down. Even Egerton's pluck gave way and he sobbed like a baby. What else could we do? Would you have had me sneak down to the Cottage and cry there by myself? Martin, I know you wouldn't – H. and I have had a hard battle with Papa to keep him from going to see her. He is so broken down by his illness and misery that even his old obstinacy – ('he's the most obstinate man I know!' as mother used to say with a rolling eye –) has left him, and he does what we ask. I begged the same thing of the Chimp, and I am thankful to say he yielded also. Only when the coffin was shut and the violet cross, that was almost as long as it was, was fastened to it, he and Aylmer and I went in and knelt down by it, and said goodbye to her in our hearts. He saw her last in all her smart clothes, going radiantly off to Christine Morrough's wedding, that is a better memory than the pale serene severe presence that had nothing of her own gay self about it. We keep saying to one another how pleased she must be about all the letters and the flowers. Only a week ago she and H. had a most vigorous argument as to whether she or Aylmer were the most popular in the country – of course H. vowed that Aylmer was, and she fought for her own hand as usual. Now she will triumph. From all round the country, from all classes there is but one voice of grief. A. said that every man and woman in Skib. came up to him, Jack Buckley who had written daily to inquire for her was crying like a baby 'your most affectionate and beloved mother, that with her own hands made a wreath to place upon my dear daughter'. That was what he said in his letter of condolence. In the village they said every door and window was shut and not a sound in the street – 'it was like there was death in each house,' said Joanna. Papa had insisted on her being buried in Castle Haven, and we can never be grateful enough to Mr. Warren. He and his men went yesterday, opened the vault, cleaned and set everything in it in order, and then both lined and covered it all with moss and white chrysanthemums. Even Aylmer who had an unspeakable horror of taking her there, said that it was beautiful and all the dreadfulness gone out of it. They carried her, in relays of six men, our tenants for the most part, and some of the coastguards, and Jack Buckley and other farmers, who don't belong to us, but wish to do honour to her memory. The tenants and the Toe Head people got out early this morning and had swept the road as clean of mud and stones as if it were an avenue, I think it was most touching of them. Jim told Ethel he never saw so much or so genuine grief. There were seventy carriages and cars and hundreds of foot people. I do so hope she knows. Can you imagine how proud she would be? I must write and tell it to Mrs. Chave. I believe that would be her first wish. I cant help laughing at her even now with the tears running down my cheeks. Do you know that the nurse hadn't been in the house for half an hour when she started her in at 'Naboth's Vinyard' and had told her all about Hildegarde, and shown her Jack's photographs? Jack Buckley was right in what he said of her – 'your most affectionate mother' – oh, dear Martin, it is a comfort to write to you, but how Hildegarde and I wish you were here. After the two of us, no one knew her in and out as you do. I am thankful to think that you stayed with her this time last year, as she was so fond of you. She was always asking me when you were coming – I am so very grateful to you for writing to poor Kinkie. I literally hadn't time. There are forty or fifty letters still to be answered, and flowers still to be thanked for. Kinkie sent a lovely wreath and the most awfully nice letter. Nothing could have been more truly sympathetic and refined too. The Canon came down to read the service with Harry Becher. He broke down two or three times. The poor boys both broke down quite uncontrollably I believe. Men have hard things to do that women are spared. She always flirted with the boys, and they adored her. They were so far far nicer to her than I was – but it is no use saying so now. After it was all over the Canon and Harry B. came over and read some prayers to Papa and Emmie and the two boys and me and gave us the Communion. The Canon's face, like Stephen's was as the face of an angel. H. was in bed and in any case she could not have borne it. It was Aylmer's suggestion and wish. I think it was very nice of him. It is very nearly one o'clock, and my candle also is burned out, but I feel better and as if I should go to sleep now – and I hear Miss Dody kicking like a little fury. I cannot praise Sylvia and Zoë and Grace enough I could never forget their kindness through it all especially Sylvia

Ever yours
Edith

H. is sleeping with me which is why I went to bed without writing to you. She is asleep now.

ed. Gifford Lewis, The Selected Letters of Somerville and Ross,
Faber and Faber, London (1989)

Violet Florence Martin (Martin Ross)

Violet Martin was born in Ross, Co. Galway, in 1862, and in 1886 met her cousin Edith Somerville for the first time which led to their literary collaborations as 'Somerville and Ross'. Their most famous works were the 'Irish R.M.' series. Violet was a keen and intrepid horsewoman; a hunting accident in 1898 resulted in spinal injuries which may have culminated in the brain tumour that caused her death in 1915.

QUEEN VICTORIA'S JUBILEE PROCESSION

Violet, in this letter to her cousin Edith, describes with characteristic humour her experiences in London on the occasion of Queen Victoria's Jubilee. References to the 'dictionary' of 'family' words include a 'carroway' – the object of a temporary devotion and 'hifle' – the energetic progress of one who has a definite object in view; 'outlying deer', unfortunately, is not listed and its meaning can only be inferred.

GUN WHARF SUNDAY EVENING AND I OUGHT TO BE AT CHURCH

JUNE 26 1887

My dear Edith

Before anything let me tell you what has just happened to me. The day is not warm, and I have gone out in a skirt without a body, and with a coat. Returning I find Arthur Paget in the drawing-room, and sinking on a chair (I had been rowing) unbuttoned my coat with a run to the very top and flung it open to its widest – and still did not see anything amiss, till the tail of my eye caught a glimpse of skin where skin does not usually show – and I sat revealed, a maid in all her charms – with Arthur opposite in strong convulsions. In that supreme moment I reflected that my stays were highly creditable – almost new, and what was visible of my combination was very neat and that my manly bosom had had its Sunday wash and altogether there were many bright features in the case – but it was awful for all that . . . Thank you very much for the dictionary in which I note some new words and many mistakes – words generally used – one or two wrong definitions etc. All these will I set in order when I come . . . Edith has remembered several of Granny's and Uncle Arthur's words – Partly obsolete but I think it is our high privilege to preserve these for prosperity – Anyhow I will take them down – One of Uncle A's which I have heard many a thousand time is 'outlying deer' a noun of multitude – meaning his various carroways. I daresay you have heard it. This lined paper is like the old times – I don't like it but have no other. I am proud of Patsey and the slaying of the rats. I didn't think he had it in him – and what shall I say of your mother and her sporting tendencies. Perhaps it may be given to me to see her engage in the past-time which is undoubtedly a fine old national one. I have long thought that nobody has principles – at least about one in a hundred – and the rest of us are just held together by conventionality and the like – being in reality ready for any crime when put at it straight. Such is the history of the downfall of the Castle Townshend moral standard. How shall I feel this summer when Aunt Adelaide sends out her invitations for her afternoon ratting party 'You will kindly bring your own rats if possible' I see Minnie arriving with a few good stable ones in a cage and laying the odds on Stinger – You made mention of a certain sketch which you kindly placed at my disposal – Never say it again – I accept with the greatest pleasure – which will probably be greater still when I see it. I like your landscapes tremendously so don't you go and give that to anyone else as you are quite capable of doing. You will not find anyone who will appreciate it more. Now that I am in the vein for saying pretty little things I may tell some things about Hamilton. All of you are delightful, he says, all of you are talented, all are hospitable – but you (unworthy slut – that I should *have* to tell it!) in your proper person form the apex. He could not say too much of your combined talent and modesty and pleasantness and wound up with 'she's as nice as they make them'. There – I cannot do better for you than that – and coming from him for whom you have confessed your affection you ought to value it. I think he was perfectly delighted with his time at Castle T. What with the weather and all of you spreading yourselves to make it pleasant for him I cannot be surprised. I have got into a maze of honeyed phrases which strange to say have given me much satisfaction to write – We missed Hamilton on his way back. He anchored at Spithead for a few hours, but as Cuthbert and Edith had not come back all I could do was go down to Arthur Paget to find out what would happen – and then discovered that *Tamar* had sailed at eleven o'clock. We had a delightful evening on board when he left this for Edinburgh – the height of eating and drinking and much high class conversation. There was a nice man called Maxwell whom he, Hamilton, chartered to entertain us – and the Captain – by name Warren – knows all the Penroses – and Castle Townshend and every mortal thing – and has an invigorating brogue – I feel it my duty to make some mention of the Jubilee – which I am bound to say was a very grand sight. As soon as we got to town we felt that we were under its spell in common with everyone in London. The town was something to remember. Countless thousands of people just walking about the street and looking about them not pretending to have any other business – Edith and I went into the Row on Monday evening, and though there were not very many people in it, the crowd at Hyde Park Corner were tremendous – all strangers and country people, come to stare at the quality going into the Park. We couldn't get through for ages. Piccadilly was wonderful from the decorations and the throngs. We walked up to the top of the hill in it and from there to Hyde Park Corner looked back at one solid block of carriages – not a move in them as far as we could see nor any prospect of a move – omnibuses and coaches all in a compact mass for a quarter of a mile. This was all the evening before – We left the house at 8 next day and even then there was a tail of people right into the street at the underground so we gave that up and footed it to Charles Street through the Park and the Green Park up to Pall Mall. I never can forget the look of the Park that morning – so beautifully dewy and fresh, with the rhododendrons so lovely that I could scarcely believe it – and the people converging through it in processions from every quarter. It felt like a sort of dream. I never knew before that feeling of a tremendous advance to a common centre – whatever way you looked there were people hurrying in – We had a squashing at the gate of Green Park but got through and fetched up at the Waterfords at about nine – There we found peace and calm, the best of good seats in the balcony, and a breakfast of the most inviting and comprehensive kind. There were about 15 other people there – just about what there was room for in the balcony. We had a perfect view as the drawing-room runs right up to Waterloo Place – or nearly. We had not the sun in our eyes, and it shone straight on the Procession as it came towards us. We ate a great deal from time to time while we were waiting – it being a crossroads we saw some most entertaining fights at corners between police and people. Several times a telegraph boy was handed across the heads of the crowd like a roll of cloth amid the greatest cheering – You know just as much of the Procession as I do from the papers. What struck me most were the Indian people, who looked like the real fine old stage princes, sparkling fit to blind you. The crown prince of Prussia, in a beautiful white uniform (poor fellow I believe he has cancer in the throat and his days are numbered) and I think perhaps the Queen herself was the finest of the whole show. You could not believe what a great lady she looked – neither could you believe how dark it is and how hard to write – no more for the present – I see that I have enthused about the Jubilee in a surprising way –

so would you if you had been there. All that remains to be said is that we hifled out to St. James Street to see them on the way back and wrestled with the filthy mob – A drunken man steadied himself against me to cheer as they passed, and though I could see nothing but the coachmen's heads I bellowed and screamed too – most refreshing it was after the lady-like reserve of the Waterford's balcony. Edith managed to get on to the corner of a chair on which there were three or four other people, and was immediately clasped round the neck by one of them, a man – who apologised – but said he must hold her round the neck or he would fall off – *She* would have fallen off if he hadn't so it was rather fortunate – Cuthbert propped her from below and while in this pleasing position her pocket was picked with great precision – She did not loose much in the way of money – but our return tickets were in the purse also her store ticket. We were nearly dead after it all but it was quite good enough. It is something to remember to have seen London off its head in the way it was – and to have heard the shouting. I believe that in the Abbey the places were ticketed a few days before 'Room here for three kings' 'Room here for 14 princes' that is to me a strange and amusing thing. Talking of the Jubilee I have received from the *Irish Times* a gift of the book of 50 poems which was presented to the Queen for light reading – Hers was bound in white satin I understand – This is rather a pretty green cloth – a poem to each page – harps and shamrocks in profusion – but not as vulgar as you would think – rather neat on the whole – I was surprised to see mine among them – Having got back the original long ago – and also surprised that they were all better than could have been expected – one or two quite good – and almost any one of them better than the one that collared the prize out of 400. It is great nobility on the Chimps part to come down with the ready as he does – and a nice healthy sentiment that he should like to have a portrait of the house – I suppose that you are doing it from the Conservatory side – It is just as well that I am not at Drishane now. I see that Sylvia would be my only companion what with the painter, the sitters and the engaged people – not that I should want a more entertaining companion I may add. I wish however that Fanny Currey had put off her visit till August. I should like to meet her – to hide about in safe corners and look on while she was with you. As to those tennis shoes I have neither seen nor heard of them – but at Richmond I may – Katy tells me that tennis is a very old-fashioned game now at C.T. Said I not well that you were all both effete and spasmodic – no healthy moderate interests – all is at fever heat, with nauseated reaction . . . By the way it is on the cards that I might bestow myself on your household about the end of July. I cannot be sure but supposing that I did, would it be the same thing to your mother? I wish I could be more exact and satisfactory, but there are wheels within wheels. Edith tells me that she humbly thanked Providence that I was not in Church tonight with her and Cuthbert. There was the most appalling back-hair sermon – too awful – she simply sat with her eyes fixed and perspiring freely – Cuthbert has a tale of a cousin of his – a very shy young man who went to the Lyceum, and during one of Irving's great soliloquies in 'Hamlet' his opera hat opened itself with a pop – that man also perspired and died a thousand deaths inwardly – which is what reminded me – This cousin went on another occasion to visit some relations with discouraging manners and an awe inspiring house. To show that he was quite unembarrassed he began to play with the favourite pug, finally dancing it round on its hind legs – it immediately threw up – and that I think ends the story. Do you know that sailor hats should be tremendously high in the crown now, and rather narrow in the brim. The people here wear them trimmed off at the back – a beastliness I think – They also wear white yachting caps – one of which I have got – and fear I am of surpassing frightfulness in it – but they look very smart on the water. Sophie Paget likes Contrayville very much, and Arthur is more or less moody and forlorn in her absence. Probably if she hated the place he would be quite happy – such are men – Mama talks of Castle T. lodgings with some confidence but I don't know what will come of it – She is almost off her head with delight about Jim coming home and I don't wonder. I don't know whether Katie has left Castle T. yet – tell me in confidence your candid opinion as to the new chastener and also in confidence what the humours of that fair fellowship have been. Evidently the present idea according to Hamilton is that the Bart hasn't even a look in – that he is tolerated in a friendly way and I do admire Katie for the way she drove those two in double harness. It amounts to inspiration. I drivel on into the smallest hours for no particular reason – except that my head is alright after being rather a bother for a few days. My address from tomorrow will be Kew Cottage – Kew – Surrey – a very delectable place just now in the way of the trees and river –

Yours

Martin

P.S. I am horrified to find it is daylight – don't give me away

DRUNKEN DRIVERS

In this letter to Edith, Violet (Martin) gives a most amusing account of her experiences in the course of her journey to the Currarevagh Ball.

29 AUGUST 1888

WEDNESDAY MORNING 5 O'CLOCK A.M.

This was not sent yesterday morning – through a mistake – and now that I have just returned from the Hodgson's dance I am going to add to it in ghastly daylight, and without embellishments the adventures which befell us last night. Geraldine as you know, chaperoned me, our vehicle was an outside car, and Jim Connor our driver. We started at 9 in the pitch darkness just before moon rise, and as soon as we got into the road remembered with some apprehension that it was the night of the Oughterard races, and the roads would be full of carts with drunken drivers. We were scarcely quarter of a mile from the gate when some thing came lumbering along with shoutings. We shouted too, all we knew, and drew into the wall, and the next moment there was a thump and crash. Up went the car on my side, the mare backed, and I found myself clawing at the coping stones on top of the wall – in fact on my hands and knees on it. Looking round I saw Geraldine and Jim safely in the road, how they got there they don't know, but they were allright and the cart had passed on.

We got the car down the bank without any trouble, and nothing daunted Geraldine and I got up, on the same side this time, giving Jim the brunt of everything we passed. With the dint of shouting and hiding in the ditch we passed innumerable cars and carts all parlattic, and were nearing Oughterard on the top of a big hill, when we heard the rattling of a heavy cart trotting towards us. We as usual made for the ditch which in this instance was a bank with a very high wall on top, but before we could look crooked that cart just rushed straight into us. The car and mare spun completely round. Geraldine somehow jumped off, so did Jim, and I not seeing exactly where to jump got onto the well – the car all the time tilting forward – and my ears full of drunken screeches. I finally managed to precipitate myself on to the muddy bank and got clear. In the shouting and darkness we could just make out that the mare had fallen partly on her side and was somehow caught in the cart. Then followed indescribable vituperation and we got the cart backed clear after much difficulty and talking ourselves hoarse. There lay the mare apparently stone dead – it was too dark to see a thing – and in the height of the confusion there came along an awful gang of roaring pedestrians. On this Geraldine and I applied ourselves to the task of climbing the wall in our ball dresses and wraps. We were not so much afraid of the drunkards as of their language, and having got up we hid behind the wall till they had passed. Emerging we found the mare on her feet without a scratch – apparently – the relief of which was enormous. The harness was in pieces, and no wonder – the shafts of the cart had gone between the belly band and the mare's body so she was lifted and swung round astride of the shaft. When the band broke – down she fell. How she was not killed is a miracle. We then made up our minds to walk on into Oughterard, about half a mile and to get a fresh harness, leaving Jim to follow with the mare. We got hold of a Ross man who was passing and made him protect us, but even with him we had a fearsome time from the drunken brutes we met – and from hobbling in thin shoes through the mud. It was a horrible walk, but once we got to Miss Murphy's hotel all was well. Jim brought in the car and mare, both perfectly uninjured and the fresh harness was jammed on and away we went for Curraghrevagh – feeling I must say a good deal battered but still undefeated – I cannot say how the whole situation was complicated by the darkness, and by my having on Mama's sealskin with a mackintosh on top of it. The feeling of suffocation when trying to climb that wall was near nightmare – and it is strange that I had a horrible dream the night before of trying to climb walls to save someone who had gone through the ice. We were of course very late at the dance arriving about number 7 but I had quite enough of it – I may say that I was tired and bored from beginning to end – though it was an awfully well done dance in every way. Somehow being knocked about tells on one, and I felt ready to subside into any corner available instead of which I dragged my weary bones through about 7 dances, and enjoyed my supper extremely – and we left as early as possible. There was no lack of people to dance with, but they were not enlivening with exception of Mr. Hanbury and another soldier of sorts – I thought the dance wanted go very much, or perhaps I did – Geraldine never lost the scared look, but otherwise was a highly creditable chaperone – Need I say that our accident was invaluable as conversation. One thing that made the evening seem interminable was occasional interludes of song from a little vulgar baritone. I could have imagined myself at Drishane for a moment, but had to realise that instead that I was talking of Trinity College to a youth with an unpleasant breath. I was somehow reminded of the Morgan's dance too – and could have found it in my heart to wish you were there – At intervals. The drive home was long and chilly but the dawn on Lough Corrib was worth looking at – I have discovered an inky bruise on my knee, another on my foot, and am generally stiff. How that Leigh ever did these things I don't know.

Mama is only middling. I don't know quite what to say of her – but Philip will pronounce. The O'Flaherties have a dance this week – nothing will induce me to go – I don't know why dancing tires me so much these times – I think it is the want of the squaw element – Does Boyle dance?

Yours

Martin

ed. Gifford Lewis, *The Selected Letters of Somerville and Ross*,
Faber and Faber, London (1989)

Constance Mary Wilde (née Lloyd)

Constance Lloyd was born in Dublin in 1858 but then lived in London. She first met Oscar Wilde at a party, given by his parents for him and his elder brother Willie, in 1881. She married Oscar in 1884; they had two children, Cyril, born in 1885, and Vyvyan, born in 1886. Their house in Chelsea was known as 'The House Beautiful'. She died, after an operation, in 1898, the year after Oscar's release from prison.

A WIFE'S DESPERATION

After Oscar was committed for trial for gross indecency in 1895, Constance was in a quandary over many things. The attitude of and the effects on the two children much exercised her. She sent them off to the continent with a French governess, to shield them as much as possible from the publicity. On the day of the committal she wrote to a palmist, Mrs Robinson, whom she and Oscar had consulted.

My dear Mrs Robinson,

What is to become of my husband who has so betrayed and deceived me and ruined the lives of my darling boys? Can you tell me anything? You told me that after this terrible shock my life was to become easier, but will there be any happiness in it, or is that dead for me? And I have had so little. My life has all been cut to pieces as my hand is by its lines.

As soon as this trial is over I have to get my judicial separation, or if possible my divorce in order to get the guardianship of the boys. What a tragedy for him who is so gifted.

Do write to me and tell me what you can.

Very sincerely yours
Constance Wilde

I have not forgotten that I owe you a guinea

A WIFE'S INDIGNATION

After Oscar's conviction for gross indecency in 1895 Constance visited
him in Reading, with much difficulty and in very degrading conditions.
She writes complaining of this and goes on to describe
Oscar's state of mind.

C/O MISS BOXWELL

12 HOLBEIN HOUSE

SEPT. 21 1895   S.W.

My dear Mr Sherard,

It was indeed awful, more so than I had any conception it could be. I could not see him and I could not touch him. I scarcely spoke. Come and see me before you go to him on Monday at anytime after 2 I can see you. When I go again I am to get at the Home Secretary through Mr Haldane and try to get a room to see him in and touch him again. He has been mad these last three years, and he says that if he saw Alfred Douglas he would kill him. So he had better keep away and be satisfied with having marred a fine life. Few people can boast of so much.

I thank you for your kindness to a fallen friend; you are kind and gentle to him and you are, I think, the only person he can bear to see.

Yours most truly

Constance Wilde

Anne Clark Amor, *Mrs Oscar Wilde: A Woman of Some Importance*,
Sidgwick and Jackson, London (1983)

THE
TWENTIETH
CENTURY

Letters from relatives, or associates, of famous men prosper during the first part of the twentieth century: women like Charlotte Frances Shaw, the wife of George Bernard Shaw – who shows in her letters that she was no mere appendage, and reveals much about herself that her husband never knew; Kitty Kiernan, who was closely involved with the dynamic Mícheál Collins; Lily, sister of the poet William Butler Yeats. Despite the fact that Yeats had long been in love with Maud Gonne she could scarcely be counted as a girl friend, though she was a considerable person in her own right.

Other women of eminence in their own right include Constance, Countess Markievicz, whose prison letters reveal a sense of humour that must have done much to help her withstand the rigours of prison life, and of course the great Helen Waddell, the medieval scholar who was bold enough to write to a former British prime minister and give him her thoughts on the coming conflict – and who, although an Ulster Presbyterian, did not find the thought of home rule for Ireland totally distasteful.

Charlotte Frances Shaw (née Payne-Townshend)

Charlotte Payne-Townshend was born in Derry, Co. Cork, in 1857, the daughter of Horace Townshend (the 'h' was inserted at his wife's behest, as was the 'Payne'), who was descended from a line of Anglican clergy in Ireland, and felt a great love of his country. Her mother, Mary Susanna, found the social life of Derry too limited for her taste and tried, unsuccessfully, to persuade her husband to leave Ireland and settle in England. In 1877 she took a house in London, where Charlotte attracted the attention of a number of men, whose proposals she turned down with consummate tact. The family travelled extensively on the continent. In 1885 her father died and Charlotte became the heiress to a considerable estate. Travelling on the continent was resumed and Charlotte attracted more suitors, none of whom interested her sufficiently. In Rome she met Dr Axel Munthe, the author who was later to write the *Story of San Michele* – to him she was attracted, but nothing came of it. In 1896, through her friendship with Beatrice and Sidney Webb, she met George Bernard Shaw. After an ardent and protracted courtship, they married in 1898. On her death, in 1943, Shaw remarked, 'I lived with Charlotte for forty years, and now I realise there was much about her I didn't know.'

THE ANXIETY OF A WIFE

In November 1898 Charlotte was becoming anxious about the lack of improvement in Shaw's foot – which had, in fact, been the proximate cause of their marrying when they did. In this letter to Beatrice she expresses that anxiety and shows her need for advice and help.

NOVEMBER 6, 1898

My Dear Beatrice,

Alas! to think that this letter only is going to meet you, instead of ourselves as I had hoped! I think you have our news up to a fortnight ago, and know . . . that we have taken another house, near here for the winter. It seemed the only thing to do, as another operation stares us in the face; and, of course, either London or travelling is impossible under the circumstances. The foot seems to have got decidedly worse in the last six weeks – but then G.B.S. has been most foolish, constantly walking on it in spite of all advice. We went up last Thursday to the specialist – Bowlby – who operated in the summer, and showed the foot to him. He said he was inclined to think that if it got fair play (that is, was kept *absolutely* quiet) it might heal still; but, if there was no change for the better, after trying this treatment for ten days, he would have to take out the whole bone, and, in consequence, take off the toe; that latter, apparently, being looked upon by the profession as a matter of no consequence.

We move into our new house – Blen-Cathra, Hindhead, Haslemere – on Saturday next if all is well. I rather hope for good effects from the change, as this is a small, stuffy house and the other has lofty, airy rooms; besides being in a better situation.

I shall be *very* glad to have you back for every reason; but, among others, for the selfish one that I long for a little advice and help from someone whose judgement and good sense I really feel that I can depend upon. I do feel rather isolated, for, though everyone makes all sorts of preposterous suggestions, no-one really gives me any feeling of confidence – the feeling I know I should have about you and Sidney if you were here. However, let's hope that long before you come the patient will be a sound man again, and there will be no need to help. Oh that —— vegetarianism!

I send you a few photographs which will amuse you. The Kodak has been a great joy to G.B.S. and nurse. . . .

The Wagner book is not out yet, but will be, I hope, in a week or so. Caesar and Cleopatra is at the 2nd. Act. I try to keep him from working as much as I can, but it is the only occupation he really cares for. Almost all books bore him, music is tiring, and seeing people more tiring still.

Graham Wallas was down here yesterday. He is getting extremely fat and prosperous looking. He described Audrey, with her large gold spectacles, kneeling in awe before the baby, hardly daring to touch it for fear of injuring it. I have not seen her as I hardly ever go up to Town.

The Fabian Executive proposes that the new vol. of essays should come out in March, and hopes for one from Sidney embodying some of your experiences. I expect the Executive meetings are a funny contrast to what they used to be when G.B.S. and Sidney were there. I find them slow – slow! I am perfectly out of patience with the Fabians (*strictly* between ourselves): from my point of view it now consists of a parcel of boys and old women thinking they are making history, and really making themselves ridiculous. Possibly this may be an exaggeration.

I will write to you at Port Said and hope there to be able to give you a more satisfactory account of our doings.

Love to you both,
Charlotte

UNIVERSITY ENDOWMENTS

Here Charlotte writes to Sidney Webb, tactfully responding to a suggestion that she should once more help financially in the foundation of the (London) School of Economics.

28TH. JANUARY, 1899   BLEN-CATHRA, HINDHEAD
                                       HASLEMERE, SURREY

My dear Sidney,

If you want University Endowments from me you should not have married me to an anarchist. I have consulted G.B.S. as to whether I should send you a thousand pounds. He tells me that if I do so it will please you and Beatrice and probably secure Mr H's* livelihood, besides providing outdoor relief for a certain number of stuttering nincompoops

---

* W.A.S. Hewins, first Director of the London School of Economics and Political Science.

who are too feeble to earn their livings in the professions. On the other hand, he declares, it will extend the present social machinery for perverting and repressing research, for replacing Webbs by Marshalls and Shaws by Paters; and it will give us the trouble of preventing the creation of some more safe Tory seats. On the whole, he cannot conceive any method by which £1000 can be made to produce more widespread social mischief than the one you propose; but such is his affection for you that he urged me to enclose a cheque sooner than disappoint you. He is, however, very much concerned about you selling out on your own account to the extent of £1000. He suggests that if you were to produce Candida with that £1000, you would not only do some real good to Society but possibly get your money back with 100% to have over for the School.

I do not enclose a cheque because the £1000 is of course conditional as I presume yours is, on the £10,000 being raised. If you can tell me when it is likely to be absolutely wanted then I can see better whether I can help with current expenses – for instance, as to the printing of the reports. G.B.S. says 'Shelves be damned: the printing is the really important thing'.

You will understand that I am not so light hearted about giving money away as I was. I shall have to save for the purpose of putting my income out of danger. You yourself refused to guarantee the National Provincial Bank for more than 20 years, and we have now reached a time of life at which we realize what a very short time 20 years is. I regret to find that G.B.S. maintains that the only guarantee one can have for an investment being for the good of humanity is a dividend. I quite realize now that it is you who are the sentimental idealist, and he the shameless man of business.

Yours affectionately,

C.F. Shaw

P.S. You will perceive by the tone of this epistle that it is a joint one, but your letter produced a great effect!

A VISIT TO THE FRONT

In this letter to her sister, Sissy, Charlotte describes a visit to the Front made by Shaw at the invitation of the War Office.

16 FEB. 1917   AYOT ST LAWRENCE

Dearest Sister,

You told me to tell you all about G.B.S.'s visit to the front.

It was the greatest possible success. Everyone was more than good to him & they extended his permit so that he was away nearly ten days instead of 3!

He went off in a bitter N. easterly gale & I thought he would have a fearful crossing. But they had a private cabin for him on the steamer & he slept, warm & comfortable, all the way over. When he got to Boulogne he was met by a Captain Roberts with a car driven straight off to the place where he was to stay. There are 3 chateaux 'Somewhere in France' (you must forgive me if I tell you things you know all about, as of course I must assume it is all news & go straight on). In one of these is housed the C. in C. & his staff. In another are the correspondents of the different newspapers – men more or less permanently out there. In the third are the 'distinguished visitors'; and there was G.B.S. I have photographs of the house, it is one of those typical 17th or 18th. Cent. big French country houses in a kind of park with a great avenue of splendid trees in front leading up to it. It appears to have been very comfortable, fairly warm & G.B.S. was quite well fed on eggs, cheese, bread & butter & lots of dried dates & figs.

He was asked the first morning what he most wanted to see, & he said Ypres. They said it was a very 'unhealthy place' but if he really must go they would see what could be done. So he was motored to Ypres. There he found the 'Town Major' who was a gigantic Irishman, who took them in charge & said 'If you want to see it all, I'll shew you, though I expect I'll be stopped by my own police – but we'll get round.' So they drove off to the principal square where the Cloth Hall is – or was. G.B.S. was very much struck by the fact that though all the houses are gutted the walls are nearly all standing – because the shells explode vertically & do almost no execution laterally. These skeletons of houses make splendid cover: the soldiers put bars of metal across & pile on top of them lots of bags of sand. This they call making an 'elephant dug-out.' Ypres is full of English soldiers living in these things, but this you are supposed *not to tell*. Why, I cannot imagine, as everyone knows the English have Ypres. Another thing G.B.S. noticed was that you go straight from the streets into the trenches. At the end of a road you will see a hole, or a door, & by that you go into the lines.

Well: when they were getting near the big square – bang! a shell exploded in front of the car! I have never been able to ascertain exactly how far in front! But anyway it frightened the chauffeur & he stopped. The Town Major yelled 'Go on man, go right on. A shell never comes in the same place twice.' So they went on. Then they saw what had been the Cloth Hall.

Then he was taken to see the Tanks, & had a ride in one! He says they go about 3 miles an hour, but when you are inside you fancy you are tearing over the ground, the engines are so powerful & make such a commotion. The great creatures will subside gracefully down the side of an immense crater, lie wallowing at the bottom, & then the most absurd thing is to see them struggling & panting up the other side. Sometimes they slide back again.

One very interesting day they took him to a place called by the Tommies Eatapples! Here there is a great camp for training the fresh men when they come out. It appears they would be quite useless if they were sent straight up to the front; they must be put into gas helmets & taught to go through gas: through the lacrimatory shell effects, smoke shells, &c. &c. Then they must be taught to go through miles of dark galleries. This seems to upset them more than anything. I think it would me!

Then there came an invitation for G.B.S. to lunch with the C. in C. & all the arrangements made for that day had to be countermanded. They had a very cheery lunch, I gather, & after lunch Sir Douglas, to the great disgust of his people, who had made other arrangements for him, said he should take G.B.S. off with him in his car to see some experiments that were being made of the new inventions. So they had a long drive alone together in an immense Rolls Royce *closed* car, & G.B.S. says it was the only time in all those bitter drives in that Arctic weather that he had a rug over his knees! They appear to have had quite a heart-to-heart talk, & to have discussed everything!

The experiments were of such things as heat shells – which are supposed to set everything on fire – & don't: & of flamme werfe (flame throwers) which are supposed to breathe out destruction – & don't. The man who was responsible for one of them said 'How amazing [annoying?], it's worked every time I've tried it until now.' And an old general called out 'It's done exactly that every time *I've* seen it.' G.B.S. said 'But it's all snow & ice & yet that shell set the furze on fire.' 'Oh' said the general, 'they soaked it in parrafin!!'

He slept that night at Amiens because it was too far to get back to his chateau & because the C. in C. said he wished him to make the acquaintance of General Rawlinson who (I understand) commands at the Somme front. G.B.S. says the old hotel at Amiens is just as it used to be, hardly any change (isn't it funny to think of: do you remember the seagulls in the garden?) In the morning he was taken round the Somme front & saw a lot of things & was under fire to the extent that one shell was sent at his party – upon which they quickly took cover. One very interesting thing he says is that the Germans are practically not firing at all at present. The English guns are going all the time – intermittently – but the enemy does not reply except just now & then. He is reserving all his munitions.

I do not gather that G.B.S. liked Sir Henry Rawlinson quite as much as Sir Douglas. He had tea with him.

That night he slept again at Amiens & in the morning drove back to his chateau, &, in the afternoon, said goodbye to his hosts there & went off to spend a night with Robert Loraine – Major Loraine – who is commanding an aeroplane squadron – (I understand, & I daresay you know, that the grades are wing, squadron, flight, in the air service, & that when Loraine becomes a flight commander he will be called Colonel.)

They live in huts, & when he got there G.B.S. really knew what cold meant. When he was dressing in the morning in his hut his money froze to his fingers! & he could not button any button without holding his fingers in a jug of hot water they brought him. The men's clothes freeze to the ground. He says Loraine is completely taken up with office work & organization, that he never flies now. His particular men do no observation or photographing, & they go up only one man in a machine. They are duellists! Their business is simply to fight. Loraine has a great, loud, braying horn, & when an enemy is reported in the air, he touches an electric button which makes this sound, & off go the men. He was shewing the horn to G.B.S. & he sounded it by accident, & in a moment, before he could say it was a false alarm, a machine was in the air. The others were not so quick & were stopped, but this unhappy hero was in the air more than an hour looking for imaginary Huns. When he came down his only satisfaction was that Loraine told him he was much pleased at his getting off so promptly.

The next day G.B.S. drove to Boulogne in Loraine's car – about an hour & a half – & there was the guest of a great friend of ours, Sir Almroth Wright (the original of Ri[d]geon in The Doctor's Dilemma) who is superintending a big hospital there; &, incidentally, making many discoveries. The men in the hospital were practically the only wounded G.B.S. saw. He seems to have escaped horrors, & saw one dead man the whole time. But he saw a regiment of men coming back from the trenches – they had been there for 16 days & were coming back for a rest – & he was greatly struck by their exhaustion. He said practically every one of them had their mouths wide open & gave the impression they were too exhausted to keep them closed.

Now I want very much to hear how your wrist is. I am practically well & can walk 2 or 3 miles then my knee gets a little stiff after that.

Let me hear if you get this letter. It would be annoying if it was lost.

The best of love to you both.

Your

Sister.

IN PRAISE OF *THE SEVEN PILLARS OF WISDOM*

Shortly after meeting T.E. Lawrence in 1922 Charlotte received from him a copy of his manuscript of The Seven Pillars of Wisdom, *asking her opinion and advice. Her assessment is quite lyrical and unequivocal.*

31ST. DECEMBER, 1922   10, ADELPHI TERRACE, W.C.

Dear Mr Lawrence,

If you've been 'mad keen' to hear about your book I've been mad keen to write to you about it ever since I read it, or rather ever since I began to read it, and I simply haven't dared. I got from it an impression of you as an Immense Personality soaring in the blue (of the Arabian skies) far above my lowly sphere, and that everything I could say in the way of admiration, or comment, or question, could only be an impertinence. But the latest developments of your career have been so startlingly unexpected, and your later letters so human, that I take my courage in both hands and send you a word.

'Now is it *conceivable, imaginable*, that a man who could write the Seven Pillars can have any doubts about it? If you don't know it is a 'great book' what is the use of anyone telling you so . . . I devoured the book from cover to cover as soon as I got hold of it. I could not stop. I drove G.B.S. almost mad by insisting on reading him special bits when he was deep in something else. I am an old woman, old enough at any rate to be your mother; I have met all sorts of men and women of the kind that are called distinguished; I have read their books . . . but I have never read anything like this: I don't believe anything really like it has been written before . . . it is one of the most amazingly individual documents that has ever been written . . .

You have been the means of bringing into the world a poignant human document, and now – have faith in the Power that worked in you. . . .

Your book must be published as a whole. Don't you see that? Perhaps little bits about the French . . . might be toned down . . . *but don't leave out the things an ordinary man would leave out*: the things people will tell you are 'too shocking.' Publish the book practically as it is, in good print, in a lot of volumes. . . .

Both G.B.S. & I have lots of experience about books & we should both *like* to put it at your service. By the way, don't call him 'Mr' Shaw!

Yours sincerely,

C.F.S.

(Mrs G.B.S.!)

Janet Dunbar, *Mrs G.B.S. – A Biographical Portrait of Charlotte Shaw*, George Harrap and Co. Ltd, London (1963)

Maud Gonne MacBride

Maud Gonne was born in 1866, in Aldershot and came to Ireland in 1882, when her father was posted to Dublin. She first met W.B. Yeats, the poet, in 1889; Yeats was overwhelmed by her beauty (as were many others). In 1890 she went to France, where she had an affair which gave her two children. Yeats proposed to her, for the first time, in 1891. She became deeply involved with Yeat's life and work, sharing for a time his interest in mysticism. She also became active in Ireland, France and America, addressing political meetings and fund-raising for nationalist causes. In 1903 she married Major John MacBride, whom she eventually divorced. (He was executed in the aftermath of the Easter Rising.) After the treaty of 1922, which she rejected, she worked for Republican prisoners and their families. She died in 1953.

AN AGRARIAN ACTIVIST SHOWS COMPASSION

Maud Gonne sincerely believed that involvement in the agrarian question in Ireland was an essential plank in the Nationalist platform. She had been campaigning in Ballina, Co. Mayo – a part of the country where the

agrarian question was particularly sensitive; partly as a result of her
compaigning, John Durkan had repossessed the house from which he had
been evicted seven years before by his landlord, Arthur Fox, Fifth Earl of
Arran, and Lord Lieutenant of County Mayo. Durkan was convicted at
the Quarter Sessions in Sligo. Maud felt personally responsible for his
predicament but feared that her overt intervention would damage his case
further. Compassion by political activists for individuals damaged by their
campaigns is so uncommon as to make this letter to her friend W.B. Yeats
a remarkable document.

NASSAU HOTEL

MONDAY [OCTOBER 1899]   DUBLIN

My dear Willie

Are you going to Sligo & when? If you are will you try and do
something for me not at all in your line. It may be quite impossible and if
so never mind. There is a poor old man called Durkan who Lord Arran
evicted under very hard circumstances. A grabber took his land but did
not live on it & one day poor old Durkan took his courage in both hands
& went back to his house, & took forcible possession, & lighted his
hearth fire. The grabber came & tried to put him out & a case of assault
was brought against Durkan at the petty assizes in Ballina but he was let
off. He went straight back & again took possession of his old home – he
was again brought up at petty sessions & this time returned for trial at
Castlebar from there he has been sent to the Winter Assizes in Sligo. The
poor old man is a most deserving case & he has a remarkably fine
character. Every effort was made to get him to swear that it was Miss
Gonne's words that made him go in, & though I certainly think they may
have had something to do with it he declared over & over again they had
not. So fearful was he of getting me into trouble over his case that he
never came to see me or asked my help while I was in Ballina. Sligo by all
accounts is a bad place to be tried in & a certain Malachy Kelly crown
prosecutor who prosecutes in this case can they say get a jury there always
to convict any man he likes.

If I openly interfered in this case I would I know only make things worse for him, but I am particularly anxious to get him off. Cannot you get your uncle or some unionist friends in Sligo to say a word in his favour – Lord Arran I believe is bitter against the old man – I am willing to pay to have him defended, but there again my name had not better appear & his advocate should not be one of the usual nationalist ones such as Harrington.

Forgive me for bothering you about this. I know it cannot interest you at all, only old Durkan has strange pathetic blue eyes with an odd faithful expression in them, which though I have only seen him once makes me want to help him –

I have been working desperately hard & am feeling rather worn out. I have one or two more meetings announced & then I must take a rest. I only go to Dublin today from Ballina. I read Evicted Tenants Restoration Scheme & must see Russell about it, on the whole I approve & will help if I can.

I saw Lady Gregory's letter on the theatre. Write & tell me what plays have been decided on. I must arrange to be in Dublin for all of them this year –

Are you writing much? I was in the room with George Moore for a few moments at Oldham's the other day, but there were many people & I did not know it till after, so did not really see him. Is his play beautiful?

I am disappointed that *Shadowy Waters* is not been given this year. When will it come out?

I wish I was out in the Transvaal the Boer victories are wonderful, how I admire those people. What a ghastly horror war is, even while I am denouncing those poor fools of Irish soldiers who are out there in England's service, a miserable feeling of pity comes which makes me sad in spite of England's defeats but as for Chamberlain & the English Cabinet & financiers responsible for this war, all the Chinese tortures invented by Mirbeau's diseased brain in his *Jardin des Supplices* would not be bad enough for them, from which very common place remarks you will see that I must be very tired & overworked & had better end this long dull letter.

Goodbye my friend, don't give yourself too much trouble about my old evicted tenant, only if you see the way to saying a good word for him to some likely unionist juror please do so. It is useless speaking to any nationalist they will be all told to stand aside. One voice in the jury would be enough I hear to save him.

> Write to me soon
> Very sincerely your friend
> Maud Gonne

REFLECTIONS ON THE IRISH REBELLION

After the unsuccessful Irish Rebellion of 1916 the British government responded with spectacular ferocity: on 3 May three of the leaders, Patrick Pearse, Thomas McDonagh and Thomas Clarke were shot after trial by court martial; four more were shot the following day and on 8 May Maud's husband, John MacBride, became the eighth. In this letter to Yeats she muses on the tragedy of Irish politics.

[MAY 1916]   COLLEVILLE

Dear Willie

Thank you for your letter & paper forwarded from Paris where we return tomorrow.

I am overwhelmed by the tragedy & the greatness of the sacrifice our country men & women have made. They have raised the Irish cause again to a position of tragic dignity. They will have made it impossible to ignore Ireland or to say that she is satisfied at the conference where at the end of the war, much will be heard about the Right of small nationalities.

If materially they have failed, & I think that failure must have been inevitable for the whole of this war has proved that inferiority of arms & scarcity of ammunition condemns the bravest to inevitable failure – their courage & determination in the cause of freedom has equalled that of any of the soldiers of the belligerants & has surpassed the courage of most of them, who are fighting poor devils because they *cannot* do anything else. Practically, & *politically* I do not think their heroique sacrifice has been in vain.

You are quite right in saying the English Government should have, after passing Home Rule, at once given power to an Irish executive & if they had this tragedy would not have happened. They would have done it, if they had been sincere but Irish parliamentarians *themselves* have told me in Paris that they considered Home Rule was betrayed & that after the war another government would rescind the Home Rule bill. I heard this opinion also from a french journalist who generally know things English pretty well, though of course it is the fashion up till now in France to say that Ireland is now quite satisfied & that England has granted her all she wants.

The disgraceful trick of trying to dishonor Roger Casement is already beginning, little notes in the French press pretending to come from a *Dutch source* couple his name with that of Eulenberg, & said that it was reported he was arrested in Germany. In Ireland at least no one will believe this.

At the beginning of the war I had a horrible vision which affected me for days. I saw Dublin, in darkness & figures lying on the quays by O'Connell Bridge, they were either wounded or dying of hunger – It was so terribly clear it has haunted me ever since. There must have been scenes like that in the streets of Dublin during the last days.

I hope to see you for I am going to try to get to London with Iseult in a week, my difficulty is always leaving the boy –

Have you news of Helen Moloney? Perhaps you will hear through the players. One feels anxious for every friend one has in Dublin –

Thank you for writing, our letters crossed, & the newspapers – I go back to Paris tomorrow.

Always your friend

Maud Gonne

eds Anna MacBride White and A. Norman Jeffares, *The Gonne–Yeats Letters 1893–1938*, Hutchinson, London (1992)

Nora Joyce (née Barnacle)

Nora Barnacle was born in Galway in 1884; she left there in 1904 and found work in a small hotel in Dublin. It was while working here that she first encountered James Joyce, and in October of that year eloped with him; they lived a rather nomadic life on the continent – in Trieste, Paris and Zurich. She bore Joyce two children, Giorgio in 1905 and Lucia in 1907. They married at a Register Office in London in 1932 – mainly, it would seem, to legitimize their children. Nora remained with Joyce until his death in 1941. She died in 1951.

A FORMAL LOVE LETTER

In this letter to James Joyce, written shortly after their first meeting, Nora, aware that her new friend had literary aspirations, writes in a very 'flowery' style – to the extent that one of Joyce's friends (to whom, rather meanly, he had shown the letter), suggested that she might have copied it from a 'letter-writing book'.

16 AUGUST 1904   LEINSTER STREET

My Dearest

My loneliness which I have so deeply felt, since we parted last night seemed to fade away as if by magic, but, alas, it was only for a short time, and I then became worse than ever. When I read your letter from the moment that I close my eyes till I open them again in the morning. It seems to me that I am always in your company under every possible variety of circumstances talking to you walking with you meeting you suddenly in different places until I am beginning to wonder if my spirit takes leave of my body in sleep and goes to seek you, and what is more find you or perhaps this is nothing but a fantasy. Occasionally too I fall into a fit of melancholy that lasts for the day and which I find almost impossible to dispel it is about time now I think that I should finish this letter as the more I write the lonelier I feel in consequence of you being so far away and the thought of having to write write [*sic*] what I would wish to speak were you beside me makes me feel utterly miserable so with best wishes and love I now close

Believe me to be ever yours

XXXXXXXX Nora Barnacle

A NATURAL LOVE LETTER

In this letter, written shortly after the 'formal' one, Nora shows herself more clearly as the warm, loving woman she was. Her style in this letter has suggested to some Joyce interpreters that she was the model for Molly Bloom in her monologues in Ulysses.

Dear Jim

I feel so very tired to night I can't say much many thanks for your kind letter which I received unexpectedly this evening I was very busy when the Postman came I ran off to one of the bedroom's to read your letter I was called five times but did not pretend to hear it is now half past eleven and I need not tell you I can hardly keep my eyes open and I am delighted to sleep the night away when I cant be thinking of you so much when I awake in the morning I will think of nothing but you

Good night till 7.P.M. to morrow eve

Nora *XXXXXXXX*

AN UNSATISFACTORY HOLIDAY

In this letter to Joyce, Nora complains that the ill-health of her children, Giorgio and Lucia, has made her holdiay in Visinada – a mountain village renowned for its healthy climate – totally disastrous. The fact that there were no shops did little to increase her enjoyment. The cryptic message at the end is reckoned to refer to Nora's gynaecological condition – specifically a vaginal discharge.

Dear Jim

I did not enjoy myself in the least since I came here Lucy has been ill all the time and when she got better Georgie took ill last night he was vomiting all night and is feverish to day I did not sleep a night since I came with Lucy every time she would look at the wild look of the place she would begin to cry she wont go to Gina so that I have to carry her about all day the food is very heavy so that's probably what upset Georgie you need not bother sending me pocket money and I dont intend to stay any longer than Monday so I hope you will kindly arrange for it I intend to go back by steamer I hope your eyes are better there are no shops here cant buy anything no more at present hoping Stannie is well

write soon

Nora

still continues

Brenda Maddox, *Nora: a Biography of Nora Joyce*,
Hamish Hamilton, London (1988)

Florence Darragh

Florence Darragh was a successful London actress and performed at the Abbey Theatre in Dublin in 1904. She was engaged – at a salary far higher than that of the rest of the Abbey players – to appear in the leading role in Yeats's *Deirdre*; her performance received good reviews.

THEATRE POLITICS

In this letter to the poet and playwright W.B. Yeats, Florence tells him of a meeting she had with Miss A.E.F. Horniman, a supporter of the theatre, who expresses to Florence some of her feeling of dissatisfaction with the way the theatre is being managed. Mrs P.C. is, of course, Mrs Patrick Campbell.

22 SEPTEMBER 1906   LONDON

Dear Mr Yeats

Many thanks for yours which of course I kept private. I'm so glad 'Deirdre' has risen & is in full flight & that everything your side is so smooth. – Now as to Miss Horniman – she lunched with me on Tuesday & in her own words burst into song from 1.30 to 5. So I listened & said about 6 sentences which resulted in her asking me to go and see her on Monday to meet a Miss Spencer who would tell me more grievances etc. She is dining here on Thursday so you see I am paying her all those ridiculous little attentions which she values so much and which she has firmly fixed in her mind none of the Irish Theatre have paid her. Of course she is in a state of seething fury about the whole thing and says she hates everything and nearly everyone apparently concerned with the Irish Theatre. However thro' it all she has a tenacious hankering after it partly hatred and partly to prove herself right in her judgement of art and acting – her views are perfectly sound & in the main she is right. My common sense tells me that. Fay is of course her obsession & one that will remain too – till he is put in the position of a paid leading actor & producer *only* of peasant plays I doubt her doing anything more for the Co. I think her difficulty could be solved later on by having a Stage-manager and let Mr Fay be Producer. But the long & the short of it is she is dissatisfied because the theatre has neither made money nor acquired réclame from the public. – If the audiences can only be worked up this winter & some money got in *and* the *General public* – I underline it because she made so much point of it – tho' she might not be willing to pay for a season in London & tour she would be certainly be more likely to contemplate it – her idea is simply to make the Dublin Theatre the nucleus – the factory – the school – for an international Theatre. Irish plays & Ireland she really now cares nothing for – but I quite see she is willing for the Irish plays legendary & otherwise to be played sandwiched in with French ones & others. I don't think the situation is desperate if taken in hand now & worked up gradually. Of course she laughed at me when I suggested that I could work up audiences, yet she really thinks I can do something tho' she wouldn't acknowledge it for worlds. We never mentioned the word countenance & I never mentioned your letter in fact I hardly spoke but we parted excellent friends tho' I had to keep a big curb on myself. The mistake has been not to pay her more attention in the business point of view – answering her letters, consulting her etc. In fact a little tact & diplomacy from Fay but now of course nothing he would or could do would alter things till he takes *apparently* a back seat. She hates not being sent all the details of the Theatre the rehearsals & dates of production etc in short she wants to be treated as a sleeping manager & not a bank – it is all very trifling but human & very feminine; Of course you know I think if you had an enterprising clever American manager who ran the whole thing & got it into ship shape a man who would put money into it arrange everything & yet be clever enough to let you all have your way as to the plays & stage etc it would be so much better. – It is the working of the machine that is so fairly apparently one thing it is certainly a mistake to call it 'The National' theatre. Everyone I spoke to in Dublin fell up against that. Surely it would be better to always call it 'The Abbey Theatre' but perhaps this is done only on the posters in Longford the word National was used if Miss H. had only put her theatre in London even small as it is there would have been none of this silly worry about names & Leagues etc. Of course one thing I cannot quite understand she says you none of you have any ambition that you all be content to go round Ireland in caravans playing your plays to a handful of people instead of becoming famous. This irritates her to death & she is in the mood to like the ordinary play that makes fame and money as she said about you having refused 'Deirdre' to Mrs P.C. but 'he would have made some money'. I did not say anything as it was useless. There is one thing I am sure you ought to try & work up the theatre and get independent of Miss H. or try to. She would fling thousands into your lap if she saw you were becoming independent. – By the way could you give me any idea of the dates you are playing in Dublin & what & when you think you will want me as I might fill in time here. I hope I haven't written too plainly but this is the situation as I see it. – I'm so glad Lady Gregory's play is getting on. – & let me know what you think about my idea of an American manager.

Yours
F. Darragh

eds Richard J. Finneran, George Mills Harper and William M. Murphy, *Letters to W.B. Yeats*, Macmillan, London (1977)

Constance Countess Markievicz (née Gore-Booth)

Constance Gore-Booth was born in London in 1868, but spent her childhood at the family house at Lissadell, Co. Sligo. She studied painting in London and later in Paris, where she met the Polish Count Casimir Markievicz, whom she married in 1900. Returning to Ireland she became involved in cultural and political activities. In 1909 she founded Fianna Éireann, a Republican youth movement. She was an ardent feminist and socialist and in 1916 was arrested and condemned to death for being an officer in the Irish Citizens' Army, founded by James Larkin, but was reprieved because of her gender. Eventually, preferring political to military means, she joined de Valéra's Fianna Fáil in 1926. She died in 1927.

THE PRACTICALITIES OF IMPRISONMENT

This letter from Constance to her sister Eva, just after her imprisonment in Mountjoy Prison in Dublin, for her participation in the Rising of 1916, shows clearly how many practical issues needed attention in her absence; it also shows her concern – born both from the care of the better sort of landlord in Ireland, few though these may have been, and her interest in socialism – for her faithful employees.

MOUNTJOY PRISON,

MAY 16, 1916   DUBLIN,

Dearest Old Darling,

It was such a heaven-sent joy, seeing you. It was a new life, a resurrection, though I knew all the time that you'd try and see me, even though I'd been fighting and you hate it all so and think killing so wrong. It was so dear of Esther to come all that long way too. Susan too, for I expect lots of people will think it very awful of her. Anyhow, you are three dears and you brought sunshine to me, and I long to hug you all!

Now to business. H—— and H—— are agents for Surrey House. They wrote to me *re* giving up tenancy, and very decently secured the house, which had been left open. The house is very untidy, as I had no time to put it straight after the police raid.

My valuables are all with a friend (silver and jewelry). I am rather unhappy about the pictures. I don't want anything thrown away. Egan —— might store those pictures hanging on the walls, and my illuminated address from the Transport Union. He has some pictures of ours already.

Don't store furniture with M——: he was a brute to his men in the strike. You'll want to insist on their bringing proper boxes for the books, as they are awfully careless. The china too wants care. Then there are the acting things. You'll probably want to buy a tin trunk or two, and get them packed with naphtha balls. There are wigs in the bottom of the kitchen press and in the cupboard half-way up the stairs. They want to be put by with care. The linen too, such as it is, wants to have the starch washed out before it is put by. If you could only catch Bessie ——, she knows the house so well and is such a good worker. There are a lot of crewel wools in the big press on the stairs: they want to be put with naphtha balls too. If someone could house the wigs and them I'd be thankful.

On the right of the fireplace in drawing-room is a sort of a desk. The same key fits it and the big brown press upstairs. One of my friends has the key. If you have not got it, pull out top drawer and push down and push lock back where it pokes through. Small centre drawer is locked: there is nothing in it.

Could Susan get my clothes and look after them for me? There is a little brown case with drawing things that Susan might keep for me. I told you that C—— and Co. are trying to let St. Mary's. I think my name should be suppressed and it should be let in yours.

Of course my household bills are not paid. C—— of Richmond Street is my grocer; F——, Rathmines, my baker; K——, butcher, and H——, oilman, are both Rathmines. I owe two coal bills: one to C——, Tara St., and the other to a man I forget in Charlemont St., on the right-hand side as you face the bridge, but close to the chemist at the corner where the trams cross. I owe also a trifle to G—— of O'Connell St. for a skirt, and to the Art Decorating Co., Belfast. But there is no hurry about any of these. Don't pay anything unless you know the bill is really mine, as people have played queer tricks, getting things on credit in my name before now.

You poor old darling. It's such a bore for you. I feel rather as if I were superintending my own funeral from the grave!

There is a very old book of music in the drawing-room. It might be valuable. If you have time, bring it to a Mr. Braid at P——, and ask his advice about selling it. I promised to let him have a look at it, as he says it is unique. I had no time to leave it with him.

I left a green canvas suit-case and a small red dressing-case with the caretaker of Liberty Hall. I've had them there some time. I dare say Peter's arrested, but he wasn't mixed up in anything, so he may be out. I left my bike knocking round the Hall too.

I miss poor 'Poppet' very much and wonder if he has forgotten me. Poor Mrs. Connolly – I wonder where she is, and if you got him from her. I do feel so sorry for her. She was so devoted to her husband. Also she has four children at home and only the two older girls working. With regard to Bessie ——: what I had in mind for her was to start her in a small way in some work after the War. She is a beautiful laundress. Of course she would want another girl with her to do accounts, etc., but you could let her know that she is not forgotten, and the ten shillings a week is only to keep her safe and happy until something can be arranged. It's much better for people to earn their own living if they can.

Poor Bridie —— ought to get a month's wages, at least. She was arrested with me. Bessie would know where she lives: somewhere in Henrietta St. If you can't find Bessie, advertise for her in the evening paper. I hope you found Mrs Mallin. I wish I knew, for it worries me so to think of her.

I nearly forgot the little Hall in Camden St. Mr C—— of Richmond St. is the landlord. If things quiet down, I'd like to go on paying the rent for them as hitherto. A little boy called Smith, living in Piles building, could find out. The landlord, of course, might know. He was quite nice.

I feel as if I were giving you such a lot of worries and bothers, and I feel, too, that I haven't remembered half. Anyhow, it's very economical living here! and I half feel glad that I am not treated as a political prisoner, as I would then be tempted to eat, smoke and dress at my own expense! In the meantime, all my debts will be paid, I live free, and after a time I suppose I will be allowed to write again and see a visitor. I don't know the rules. But do try to get in touch with Mrs. C——, Mrs. M——, and Bessie —— for me. I would be sorry for any of them to be hungry, and I would be sorry too if they thought I had forgotten them, for they were friends.

By the way, the garden seat and tools might be of use to Susan. There are a few decent plants, too, which she could take if she likes, and a couple of decent rose-trees.

Now, darling, don't worry about me, for I'm not too bad at all, and it's only a mean spirit that grudges paying the price.

Everybody is quite kind, and though this is not exactly a bed of roses, still many rebels have had much worse to bear. The life is colourless, the beds are hard, the food peculiar, but you might say that of many a free person's life, and when I think of what the Fenians suffered, and of what the Poles suffered in the 'sixties, I realise that I am extremely lucky. So don't worry your sweet old head. I don't know if you are still here, so I am sending this to Susan to forward.

I hope that I shall live to see you again some day and I shall live in hopes.

With very much love to you three darlings.

I can see your faces when I shut my eyes.

EXILE

On her transfer from Mountjoy Prison in Dublin to Aylesbury, Constance writes to Eva contrasting the 'homeliness' of Mountjoy with the strangeness and loneliness of Aylesbury.

Dearest Old Darling,

The one thing I have gained by my exile is the privilege of writing a letter, but there is very little to say, as I do not suppose 'an essay on prison life' would pass the Censor, however interesting and amusing it might be!

What you have called 'my misplaced sense of humour' still remains to me, and I am quite well and cheerful.

I saw myself, for the first time for over three months, the other day, and it is quite amusing to meet yourself as a stranger. We bowed and grinned, and I thought my teeth very dirty and very much wanting a dentist, and I'd got very thin and very sunburnt. In six months I shall not recognise myself at all, my memory for faces being so bad! I remember a fairy tale of a princess, who banished mirrors when she began to grow old. I think it showed a great lack of interest in life. The less I see my face, the more curious I grow about it, and I don't resent it getting old.

It's queer and lonely here, there was so much life in Mountjoy. There were sea-gulls and pigeons, which I had quite tame, there were 'Stop Press' cries, and little boys splashing in the canal and singing Irish songs, shrill and discordant, but with such vigour. There was a black spaniel, too, with long, silky ears, and a most attractive convict-baby with a squint, and soft Irish voices everywhere. There were the trains, 'Broadstone and Northwall' trams, and even an old melodeon, and a man trying to play an Irish tune on a bugle over the wall! Here it is so still and I find it so hard to understand what anyone says to me, and they seem to find the same trouble with me. 'English as she is spoke' can be very puzzling. One thing nice here is the hollyhocks in the garden. They seem to understand gardening here. There is a great crop of carrots, too, which we pass every day, going to 'exercise' round and round in a ring – like so many old hunters in a summer.

I had the loveliest journey over here. My escort had never been on the sea before and kept thinking she was going to be ill. I lay down and enjoyed a sunny porthole and a fresh breeze. There was a big air-ship (like the picture of a Zeppelin) cruising about when we arrived. I was awfully pleased, as I had never seen one. I do so long to fly! Also I'd love to dive in a submarine.

I dreamt of you the other night. You had on a soft-looking dark blue small hat, and it was crooked. You had bought tickets and three donkeys, and you were going to take Esther and me to Egypt, of all places! When I woke up I had to laugh, but it was wonderfully vivid. Look it up in a dream-book. I have dreamed a good deal since I was in jail and I scarcely ever did so before.

I'd love to show you all the doggerel I wrote in Mountjoy, though I know you'd only jeer – in a kindly way. I love writing it so, and I've not lost it. It's in my head all right!

When is your next book coming out, and the one with my pictures, if it ever does? They were very bad. I can do much better now. I was just beginning to get some feeling into my black and white when I left Ireland. I made quills out of rooks' feathers that I found in the garden. They are much nicer than most pens: you can get such a fine, soft line.

My darling, I repeat – *don't* worry about me. I am quite cheerful and content, and I would have felt very small and useless if I had been ignored. I am quite patient and I believe that everything will happen for the best.

One thing I should enjoy getting out for, and that would be to see the faces of respectable people when I met them!

I don't like to send anyone my love, for fear that that most valuable offering would be spurned. I expect, though, that Molly has a soft spot for me somewhere. Very best love to Esther and to Susan and all the 'rebelly crew,' if ever you come across them.

Do go to the Transport Union Headquarters if ever you go to Dublin. They'd all think you were me, and they would love to see you and you could tell them about me.

Send me a budget of news and gossip, when you can write, about all my pals and my family, and anything amusing at all.

Yours,
CON(VICT 12).

ed. Esther Roper, *Prison Letters of Countess Markievicz*,
Longmans, Green and Co., London (1934).

Catherine (Kitty) Kiernan

Catherine Brigid, or Kitty as she was called, was a native of Granard, Co. Longford, where her parents, who died in 1908 when she was aged sixteen, owned the Greville Arms, a model family hotel in the main street. It was in 1917 that she first met Michael Collins, or Mícheál, as he preferred, when he stayed in the hotel to assist Joseph McGuiness in fighting a by-election. Shortly afterwards he was arrested, and while on bail went on the run. Kitty's love for Collins continued to grow, through his political and military vicissitudes, until his death in an ambush in 1922. She died in 1945.

LOVE AND INEXPERIENCE

In this letter to Mícheál Kitty reveals her growing love for him but confesses her inability to cope with the strength of her feelings. It is the kind of letter that many people have, at one time or another, felt like writing.

KITTY, TO MÍCHEÁL, WEDNESDAY NIGHT, RECEIVED 10 FEBRUARY 1922.

My own lovie,

It is just 7 o'c and I've said good bye to the little shop for the day. One of the girls has a cold and was in bed today, so with Maud away I had to take the girl's place. Have just come in here and am writing to you before I have my tea. If by any chance you should come to-morrow this letter won't go, but if you don't, you will get it. How I wish you were here, ducky. I think I'd be nice to you, at least I'd do my best. You say I am very nice 'sometimes', but sure I don't ever get a chance of being nice to you.

I pity myself sometimes that I am so queer. I long to be all that I might be to you, but for these little fits. I will try so hard to overcome them because I know I'd be much happier if only I could be my real self with you. (This seems to be the beginning of a little book entitled 'The Secrets of the Heart'! However, I am in the mood for talking to you.)

Of course, I am much too sensitive, and too highly susceptible to anything you might or might *not* say, or to any of your actions. Lots of it may be imagination on my part, and it is I who suffer most perhaps, although I know it is hard on you too. While it lasts I get miserable. For instance, in Dublin at times you made me feel almost uncomfortable. I didn't know where I stood with you. I found myself wondering. You were, I know, overworked and tired. If only I could have left you alone, to yourself, until you recovered, but time seemed so precious from my point of view, and I hated not being absolutely with you, while with you. I was entirely at your mercy, lived for the time when we would meet again. All the days seemed empty until I had you. Then I was disappointed. Had I not set myself out to devote *all* my time to you, it would have saved the position and made it more comfortable for both of us really. But there's where I have to learn a lot. There is where I am young and inexperienced. I should have made a programme for myself, and not be entirely depending on you. But then the point comes in. To love you *at all* is a nuisance to you. I told you so before – no half-measures with me. (I do not tell you how I feel often, and try to overcome my feelings for you, ducky, with the obvious result.) But would it not be better in the long run if I could succeed now. There's the position.

On the *other* hand, I almost shudder at the thought of the strength of my love, what I do believe I am capable of feeling and that, without you, life held nothing for me. Nobody mattered to me, not even myself, if you were not with me. In other words it would mean just living for you. Then how to live *best* for you. To do justice to myself as well as to you is also a puzzle. Because I'll feel that if I do it for myself, it's for you. Every little thing would be for you as well as for me. I'd naturally like to feel happy, because I do believe that mood would affect you and make you happy. I think perhaps my unhappiness is purely from being run down etc., and that, please the Lord, can be altered when I get right away from the present surroundings, the horror of everything staring one in the face, and no way out of it.

And now I'll finish. I long for the time when I can be (as I used always to be) gay and light-hearted, and then I'll make big worries seem small, and small things nothing at all, and you will be my little world. I mean my world would be you, first. This is no foolish talk or imagination. And if only the day comes soon when I can thoroughly understand you, and even when, like in Dublin, I won't be so greedy, wanting you, wanting you, always and ever wanting you. And isn't it something nice for you to dream about, no matter how complicated it might at the time become?

But not so pleasant at the time for

Your Kit

A PROPOSAL

Kitty's love for Mícheál continued to grow and she increasingly desired the ultimate ambition of marriage and 'living happily ever after'. The 'Miss McC' is Myra McCarthy of Grianán na nGaedheal, while Mr Barry is a childhood friend of Kitty's.

KITTY, TO MÍCHEÁL, MONDAY NIGHT, RECEIVED 28 FEBRUARY 1922.

My own dear Mícheál,

There is no post going out to-day, and I am so sorry that you can't have this in the morning. The train was too crowded to write a letter last evening. Larry, Paul etc. were on train also. We all got home safely, T.G.

Am thinking ever since how you are getting on. Of course, my coming home had the inevitable result. Why did I come, why didn't I stay with you? But really I did feel helpless while there. I could do absolutely nothing for you, and the idea in my mind all the time was that you would be better alone. There is not – nor should there be – any necessity to tell you how I felt about you. I was a bit of an invalid myself, and so didn't feel inclined to tell you all the nice things that I felt and were left unsaid. You will understand and forgive your own little me. *I* felt all the time that I'd love to be physically able to wrap you up in a big rug or something and carry you off to somewhere nice, far far away from 44 – yes, from 44, very far – to where there was wooded scenery, and large windows, the birds singing, and me in good humour, and where you could get a little breeze from the sea – or even the smell of the sea – and then a whole lot of other little things, the small things which also count.

I think I would be happy to-day if I knew that you had gone to even a nice nursing home, and that you slept all last night. I don't consider that you will really do Ireland or the people of Ireland any good by killing yourself working. You only do them an injustice. You are the one that, by living for Ireland, helps her. And then the injustice you will do me, sweetheart. We both clearly understand that any pain you may have is also mine, and any pain you might endure through not sleeping is just the same as if I were suffering. Your worries are my worries, your joys are my little joys, your happiness mine. When you are happy I am happy, no matter what I may say or pretend.

Unfortunately I amn't always my real self with you, but I do feel that, wherever I am my real self, you love it best of all. It is that which appeals most to you. I am confident of this; in other words I have confidence in myself. I keep keeping it reserved for you which unfortunately is a mistake sometimes – not to give the rosies all the time – but there is something strange in me which sometimes makes me find it hard to understand myself. It really is Reserve. All my life I was a little like that with my nearest and dearest, tho' to those who don't really know me, I appear quite the opposite. It's a case of what I read being true. How little we know of those we know a lot, and what a lot we know of those we know a little.

Ever since I came back I have been thinking of your suggestion, and I went to the chapel tonight to pray for you and during that time thought that making the little sacrifices are no use if I couldn't make the big ones, and so it's June, D.V. Now I don't mean it's really a sacrifice in that sense, but just putting it off until I'd be ready also, etc., etc. Why not do the duty which lies nearest to me – to both of us – and be married in June? And so *Now* I have proposed to you! Are you satisfied? My weak inclination might be to put it off from month to month, but what I suggest is far the best for you, for me perhaps, and for both of us. I'll do my best to be good and strong by June D.V. and then you will at last have a responsibility; but I only want to be your little pet, your little child, your real pet, and, of course, your Duckie. That should come first, at least the way you say it. I want to be a million things to you.

I have heaps of little things to tell you when we are together, and I do believe it will be all I want if only I keep strong. That seems sometimes a little barrier. If it was got over, I feel I could do anything, and my longing would not be in vain. You know my longing, that I may fulfil all the part in life's little drama successfully for you and me. It's a big lot to expect. Nothing like looking for the big things anyway.

I must stop and say good night as I feel tired and sleepy. Will post this on first post tomorrow. You may yet get it sometime tomorrow. I send you a magazine I had in the train. If you are still in bed, read what amused me.

Will go to town on Wednesday, D.V., and please do your best to rest until then. Then a week somewhere – not sometime.

It's a great idea writing single pages, looks volumes this letter. Must write to Miss McC. my thanks.

> By bye, my lovie.
>
> From your little sweetheart, lovingly,
>
> Kit

Travelled with my friend Mr Barry again last night. He is one of the nicest boys I have ever known. I have asked him to visit *us* sometime.

Write me something nice to cheer me. Something about your own dear self. You are all and only you. I am not extra nice to you when you are in bad shape. Love, goodbye, my lovie, lovie.

ed. León Ó Broin, *In Great Haste: the Letters of Michael Collins and Kitty Kiernan*, Gill and Macmillan, Dublin (1983)

Lily Yeats

Lily, born in 1866, was one of the sisters of the poet and playwright W.B. Yeats. She was much involved with Cuala Industries – which included the Cuala Press.

FAMILY TENSION

In this letter to her famous brother, Lily tells him of the tension between her and their sister, Lolly. Maria Brien and Rose (Hodgins) were their servants; Ruth (Pollexfen) their cousin. The other women mentioned were employees of Cuala Industries.

[CA. FEBRUARY 1924]   LONDON

My will wishes

Maria Brien must be got rid of. She is pilfering and drinking, has been most unsatisfactory of late. She is also bad for Lolly and tormenting to Rose. I know I cannot face my life with her or Lolly *ever* again. My idea would be to move Lolly into a small flat or house with *two extra* rooms for the Press, and let her do her office work in her own sitting room and keep Rose with her. She would want Eileen, Essie, and Kathleen, for hand colouring at Xmas she could get extra help.

Keep embroidery in one room at 82 with Sarah May Annie Sissie and Lizzie. Latter might not come so far but she is good. May may get married and so I suggest keeping Sissie and Lizzie to take her place. Sarah to be made head girl. Lena is at present ill and is not really important, might be got for extra rush.

I feel this is a break which had to come and I feel I ought to take advantage of it and make a complete separation from Lolly, for life with her for the past twenty years has been torture. Dr Goff knows she is incurable, and having suffered so much and gone through so much with her that I feel it is impossible ever to think of living with her again. Her jealousy is one of the greatest curses. It is not only with Ruth that this jealousy arises but with anyone I am friendly with. If I walk down the road with Phillida (Miss Boston) she won't speak to either of us all evening.

To give an example of her suspiciousness. One day I told her I was going up to see Dr Goff and she made up her mind that I was going to see Ruth and rang up Dr Goff and finding to her surprise that I was with him gave him some trifling message for me. Remember that I had only left the Industry twenty minutes before this.

I do not want Willy or George to think from this that we led a cat and dog life. It never came to that, for many years ago I saw no escape and I faced it out and decided I would never be the cause of a scene with Lolly. I felt nothing would ever be gained by as it were 'having it out with her.' I said to myself, 'She is incapable of realising what she is either saying or doing,' but I also said to myself, 'She is getting less and less sane, and she is gradually killing me.' But again I thought I can do nothing as I have to live my life with her. And now there is hope. I want to thank Willy and George for this ease of body and mind they have given me. I feel most grateful to them, it is like the coming true of a dream to me. Whether I recover or not while lying in bed I will get great happiness out of thinking that there can be a life for me of the freedom that I have all my life longed for. I never wanted very much from life. At any rate I didn't get it. But I must say I've laughed a great deal more than I have cried.

I would like Willy George Jack and Cottie to look after Rose. She is very affectionate and very timid and easily made unhappy and easily made happy – and if it so happened that with Lolly she became unhappy I would like them to try and get her to someone like the Mitchells. She has been very faithful to us, and must not be left.

[On verso of page 1 is written, to be added after the words 'Lena is at present ill and is not really important':]

The girls can *copy* any stitch and are very reliable. Sarah I would like to be head girl. Cottie Ruth and George could carry it on most successfully. These suggestions may be impossible. The other idea would be to sell Cuala and give Lolly an annuity. If I recover I could live for at least two years with friends picking up health again.

FAMILY MATTERS

In this letter to Willy, Lily makes whimsical allusion to his famous poem 'The Lake Isle of Innisfree', and speculates about family history – remember that 'Pollexfen' was the surname of the cousin

Ruth referred to above. She goes on to give a rather bizarre insight into the attitudes to the Famine displayed by some landlords, though she does indicate the sincere concern shown by others.

1 SEPTEMBER 1938   DUNDRUM

My dear Willy–

I hear that the Land Commission have bought the Hazelwood property excluding Innisfree. The woods and house are I think to be used by the Forestry Dept – but Innisfree – will be put up notices – this way to the 'Bee glade – because of the bee, anyone interfering with the bee will be severely dealt with.' 'The beans must not be eaten. They are the property of the Land Commission' etc., – etc.

I am trying to find out more about Anne Pollexfen, Drake's daughter. There are Drakes in Ireland descended from the Admiral's brother, and Miss Overend, a friend of mine, knows them well and is going to ask them. She thinks Admiral Drake was twice married, but that there were no children of either marriage. I'll tell you if I hear any more.

I am so glad the Abbey Festival was a success. I don't think the English Press was good. Anything I say 'Statesman' etc. the notices were written by disgruntled Dubliners with scores to pay off. I would personally have liked to get the opinions of some English critics.

I enquired for you all morning from Mary. George was at the Dentist, poor creature, Mary says you are all well.

Aunt Jenny is I think just fading out, but is said to be better this morning. She was born in 1846 in the midst of the famine when our grandparents drew down the blind before they sat down to a meal. Any moment the face of starving men or women might look in at the window, and they were living on just the bare necessities, and working hard at relief work. Grandfather Yeats and the grandfather of the present Archbishop Gregg were sent together preaching through England to collect money for relief.

Gregg's grandfather was such an eloquent preacher that it is said the congregation waited outside St. Paul's and cheered him as he came out. His grandson is a preacher without fire – rather depressing, but looks fine in his black and crimson robes.

I hope you are feeling fairly well.

With love from

Your affectionate sister

Lily Yeats

eds Richard J. Finneran, George Mills Harper and William M. Murphy, *Letters to W.B. Yeats*, Macmillan, London (1977)

Helen Waddell

Helen Waddell was born in 1889 in Tokyo, where her father was a Presbyterian missionary. Her earlier education was in Belfast, where she graduated from Queen's University before continuing her medieval studies in Oxford and later in Paris. Her best-known works are *The Wandering Scholars*, published in 1927, and *Medieval Latin Lyrics*, published in 1929, as well as her novel *Peter Abelard*. She died in 1965.

HOME RULE

In this letter to her life-long friend and benefactor, Dr Taylor, a missionary in India as Helen's father had been in Japan, written in late 1919, Helen expresses her views on the Irish Rebellion and on the subject of Home Rule for Ireland. They may seem extraordinarily liberal for a Presbyterian woman of Ulster stock and upbringing – but Ulster Presbyterians had not and have not been as inexorably Unionist as they are frequently made to appear. In any case Helen Waddell was a remarkable woman with a very definite mind of her own.

Your letter has just come in. You *are* dear to write so frankly: and I'll be frank too.

Listen: when the American colonies declared their independence, after not one hundredth part of the oppression this country received, was it treason? No. But it would to this day be treason, if it had failed.

If there had been no Great War: if two hundred years from now Alsace-Lorraine had risen against German rule, would it have been treason?

If three hundred years from now, Belgium, overrun by a triumphant Germany had rebelled, would it have been treason? If, her language gone, half her country settled by Germans from across the Rhine (many of whom, however, became imbued with the Belgian spirit), but nevertheless governed equitably enough according to Teutonic ideals, she had continued to conspire, to keep alive the Belgian nationality, the hate of the conqueror, the passion for her own individuality, would it have been the malignant outworking of the spirit of evil, or the unconquerable, unquenchable 'seed of fire' which makes a man love his own country and his own children as he cannot love the alien?

The cases, you will say, are not parallel. They never are, quite. But they are going in the same direction.

One *can* be a Home Ruler, and loyal to the greater issue as well. Witness the Redmonds and Professor J.M. Kettle, and hundreds of less-known Irishmen.

I'm sorry I hurt you by telling you that about my father. But you know, it was his passion for lost causes, for 'the under dog', that makes me love him.

Dear, how *can* you possibly feel as we felt, he and I? You are English: you are of the governing nation. I see the same incapacity in Gregory.

You liken the cleavage to that between Cavalier and Roundhead. The issue there was 'government by consent of the governed': and the 'rebels' won. Only for that, they would be traitors still. It is the same issue still.

Ireland, given a Home Rule parliament when the electorate of the three kingdoms decreed it, would have given its blood like water. Sinn Fein had no love for Germany, except as a means to an end. Dear, *have* you forgotten the Ulster papers before the war? But then you didn't read them, of course, in India. The half-veiled references to German aid, that became frank outrage in wilder oratory. Do you not know that Ulster armed itself with German rifles?

What Sir Edward Carson did was to break down the hold that constitutional government had at last won in Ireland. He proved that a threat of physical force could paralyse 'government by the will of the majority'. English papers actually commented on the contrast between the red fury of Ulster and the apathy of the rest of Ireland, as proof that Ulster was much more in earnest *against*, than the rest of Ireland *for*.

Do you know that speeches on behalf of the Ulster position, collected in book form, are now suppressed as anarchic in tendency in Ireland? And by some of the very men who made them?

Ulster never feared religious persecution for itself: it used the case of the Protestants in the South and West as its strongest arguments. It must protect them, who could not protect themselves. It was offered partition: in five minutes the scattered remnant was thrown overboard, to make what terms it could, while Ulster grasped at a chance of setting up a sort of city-state. That action made the Ulster Covenant so much waste paper.

Another thing: you speak of Parnell's morals: 'these by thy gods, O Israel.' There is a monument in London to a greater than Parnell, greater even in sin, for his was a double adultery. Parnell had no wife, and Nelson had. And I do not think it likely that Parnell would have left the name of the woman in his will, to 'the care of a grateful nation', as Nelson left the name of Lady Hamilton. For this reason – that Parnell was dealing with a nation whose attitude to the marriage bond is infintely more exacting than the English. Curiously, Gregory was talking of it the other day. 'Parnell would never have made shipwreck' he said, 'if his supporters had not been in the main Irish Catholics. And adultory is a thing they will not bear.'

But, dear, it only vexes you and vexes me. Put it this way: I'd be insane to discuss 'Home Rule for India' with my knowledge. I can only wish that Tagore had not had to renounce his title as a protest against the flogging in public of educated men. That I was sorry to hear: but I recognize that a Government in a terrible situation acts terribly, and does things it might not in cooler blood. Anyhow, I have no knowledge. I only know that my faith in the fairness of British administration is very great.

But here I know a little: and more than that, I feel.

> My father and mother were Irish,
> And I am Irish too.
> I bought a wee fiddle for ninepence,
> And it is Irish too.

All the same, I have no hatred for England: I've an immense liking for it: and for certain Englishmen, a great deal more than liking. I don't call them tyrants, and I don't call the Easter 'rebels' either martyrs or traitors.

I suppose I'm a hopeless trimmer. Just as my head was with the Roundheads, and my heart distinctly Royalist.

Does it matter? Saintsbury and Gregory, two of my best friends, are Tories *in excelsis*: Saintsbury's Toryism is almost a joy to me, it's so complete. I am quite convinced that he is a Jacobite in fact.

Dear – the men who died for the Pretender – were they 'traitors'? And upon my honour, scores of the men who died in Easter week died 'for a dream's sake'. And yet, to you, with your traditions, I see that they *must* be traitors. So be it.

I come back and back to the catalogue of the Twelve Apostles. 'He chose . . . Simon the Zealot' (as who should say, a man who had been 'out' in Easter week)' . . . Matthew the Publican.'

And by tradition, it was Matthew who had denied his birthright who wrote the Gospel for the Jews.

But I see that mine is an attitude you can't well understand. But remember the tradition among us, that one of us was hanged for treason in '98, and that the Governor of the Jail where he was hanged was a kinsman of his own.

My dear love to you. And remember, dear heart, before you worry over me too much, that we're nearly all Radicals in youth!

WAR

In this remarkable letter, written in 1939, on the eve of the Second World War, Helen addresses the former British Prime Minister, Stanley Baldwin, and urges him to take firm action against the bullying tactics of Nazi Germany; in the event it was, of course, Winston Churchill who formed a coalition War Cabinet, without Stanley Baldwin.

My dear S.B.

I sent you a wire this morning in a kind of desperation, after reading Hitler's own phrase at Berchtesgaden: that he would solve the Sudeten affair 'nun der Preis eines Weltkrieges'. I had believed until now that a threat only stiffened our backs. Now I am being silly and quoting *Antony & Cleopatra* –

'I never saw an action of such shame',

and

'I'll bathe my dying honour in that blood
Will make it live again'

and then remembering bitterly that I have always said I cannot see the young men go – *twice*.

Yet if one is not a complete pacifist, one knows that to let a bully threaten and not call his bluff ends in the slavery that John of Salisbury calls 'imago mortis'. And at the Youth rally at the German Embassy two nights ago they got drunk enough to say that they had never dreamt England wouldn't call their bluff – that they weren't ready to take us all on. Chamberlain is a decent man, but he is curiously innocent.

But, dear S.B., I don't want the arbitrament of blood if it can be helped. I do want England to be made to feel that she is a democracy. At the moment, most intelligent people feel that Chamberlain is virtually dictator – that we are a totalitarian state with none of its advantages. It seemed – but forgive the 'female phranzy' – madness to me not to summon a Parliament on an issue like this. I have a horrid fear that Chamberlain is relying on the terrible passivity of the English before a *fait accompli*, though they'll fight like tigers if the issue is before them, still unresolved. The attitude of 'Mother knows best' doesn't survive the nursery: and since the Anglo-Italian agreement no one trusts his wisdom.

Can't you come back, if not as P.M. (though in the Lords you would escape the sheer nagging of the job), then as Lord President, with Eden as P.M. and have a real Coalition cabinet as in the War, with Attlee and Sinclair and *both* Morrisons – the thing has gone far beyond party advantage.

I speak like a fool. I would be better employed translating John of Salisbury's strange wisdom. I'll append a piece of it for your meditation.

There is one beautiful thing – the outraged honour of the young men – not the intellectuals – people like my houseman (who does everything from cooking very nicely to petting the kitten and cutting the grass), and the taximan round the corner, and the stocky little man who came for 'empties' this morning, and whom I waylaid to hear his views. 'I'm a man has got no education, Miss, and maybe I don't know the rights of it. But I'm ashamed to be an Englishman.' I haven't heard that since the Black and Tan stories began coming over to England in 1921.

Anyhow, thank heaven you are home again.

My love and duty always,

Helen

John of Salisbury goes to you later.

D. Felicitas Corrigan, *Helen Waddell – A Biography*,
Victor Gollancz, London (1986)

One hardly expects there to exist published letters from the second part of the twentieth century. Indeed there would have been no such entry in this book had not a friend shown me a copy of Pure Heart and Enlightened Mind – The Zen Journal and Letters of an Irish Woman in Japan *by Maura Soshin O'Halloran. I found it completely enthralling and could not resist the temptation to include a couple of examples, written to her family in a style that combines the homely and the spiritual to an astonishing degree.*

Maura O'Halloran (Soshin)

Maura O'Halloran was born in 1955 in Boston, Massachusetts, the eldest of six children; despite her American birth her father, Fionan Finbarr O'Halloran, was a native of County Kerry and much of Maura's life and education was in Ireland; she graduated from Dublin University in 1977. During her college years she was deeply involved in social work, especially with drug addicts and the very poor in Dublin. Her interest in Japan, encouraged by a family friend, developed during the early 1970s and in 1979 she began training in Zen at the Toshoji Temple in Tokyo and the Kannonji Temple in Iwate. In 1982 she received the transmission of her roshi; but was tragically killed in a bus accident in Thailand six months later.

CHRISTMAS IN A BUDDHIST TEMPLE

Two months after her acceptance into the Temple in Tokyo Maura writes to her family to tell them of her rather bizarre first Christmas and the loving sympathy of the monks. She also describes her earliest experiences, and the public reaction, as a practising Buddhist.

JANUARY 13, 1980

Dear Family,

Happy birthday to my favourite brother in this whole world. Wish I could be with you. You've gone and grown up behind my back. Hope you like school and you're not showing off too much with all A's. An A– here or there would be good for the other kids. Right?

How was the Christmas for yis? I missed you. Christmas Eve was very cold and glum without a sprig of holly or a sniff of turkey. I was feeling decidedly on the wrong side of the Pacific. Word went around the monastery that I was down in the dumps, and they all rallied round. One monk did my chores for me. Another one wrapped me in a big woolen coat (it was freezing), popped headphones on me and played tapes, his prize being hymns from Notre Dame. The abbot went out and bought a 'Christmas cake,' and the cook bought champagne. They were going to give me a Christmas party. Well, it was the funniest looking Christmas party I ever saw. Five monks and the cook huddled in the cold around four wooden benches. The plastic tree and yule log looked strange sitting on a 'Christmas cake' of whipped cream and fresh strawberries. They lit birthday candles on the cake. Don't all Western cakes have candles? But they didn't know what to do with them, so they turned off the light and patiently waited for the candles to melt down. Then they played 'Silent Night' in Japanese and took turns singing English songs. Then Tetsuro-san leaps to his feet in full monk's regalia, hips swinging, and in choppy Japanese accent he does his rendition of Elvis Presley. Then there was 'Home, home on the lange.' Great cheer all around, though you could see everyone's breath as each sang his song. The party ended at 8:00; we all had to be up at 4:30. It wasn't quite Christmas, but it was certainly the Christmas spirit.

All the while there was the build-up to going begging this month. A couple of days before we were to leave for the north, one of the monks came to my room with an armful of bandages.

I asked what they were for. 'Your wounds,' he replied solemnly. We both consulted our dictionaries to make sure bandages and wounds were the right words. They were. I closed the door and wondered just what I'd let myself in for this time. I felt as if I was going off to war.

I've hit the news again. Aren't you glad it's not a demonstration this time? Everyone was amazed at a girl and a foreigner going begging. It looks hard, walking for hours through the snow in straw sandals (with socks), chanting and ringing a bell. 'Severe training for a boy,' they say, 'but for a girl?' and their slanted eyes widen. So they interviewed me on TV; then the newspaper for this prefecture came around. I don't know what they wrote. The reporter couldn't speak English, so one of the monks told him all about me. Suddenly I had a public. People in buses would wave and point; children followed me in the street; people chased me to put money in my bowl. Today the newspaper came round again. There was such a response that they want another article.

It's funny, the begging isn't bad at all. I wear literally ten layers of clothes and once the fingers and toes are numb, you don't feel a thing. It's nice walking through the streets singing at the top of your lungs. It's like going Christmas caroling every day. Then the little wooden door rattles and slides across, and an old woman, bent over, clutching her shawl, shuffles in the snow to drop whatever she can in your bowl, then bends her head reverently waiting for the blessing I can't give.

Most days families from the town invite us to lunch. It's a big occasion for them, and they go all out. We wear our ceremonial dress. They put a feast before us. I'm trying all kinds of Japanese delicacies I could never have afforded otherwise. They're on their knees pouring out their thanks to us again and again for coming to their homes. If you could see the old women with tears rising to their eyes, holding the abbot's gown and thanking him. It's so strange to be in this respected position. I'm not used to it in my own culture, let alone this one. Fellows my own age passing in the street who normally would try to chat me up instead join their hands as if to pray and bow deeply. All the while I'm trying to keep a straight face.

This amulet that I'm enclosing was especially commissioned by the abbot for you. It is a New Year's blessing to bring health and happiness to the home. On the right is our name, on the left is the temple and the monk that wrote it (the same one that did Elvis on Christmas Eve). They say it should be hung in a special place.

When you mentioned coming to Japan, I must say, selfishly, I'd love you to come over; it'd be great to see you, but in fact if you're going to spend the money you'd get better value anywhere else. Prices are ridiculous. $20.00 for a steak, $13.00 for a melon, $1.50 for a cup of coffee . . . it's all true. But then you could eat tofu and mandarins and drink green tea instead. Little was left of old Japan after the war; now it's mostly ugly concrete rabbit warrens, but for me it's grand because I'm living in thirteenth century Japan and it's fascinating. But I must say, of all the countries I've been to, modern Japan would be low on my list of 'must come back to's.'

However, I'd still like to see ya.

Love, M.

JAPANESE PROPOSALS, THEATRE AND WEDDINGS

In this letter to her mother, Maura describes an unexpected proposal (and her successful effort to disengage herself), her experience of Japanese theatre and her attendance at a wedding.

APRIL, 1981   KANNONJI, IWATEKEN

Dear Mum,

. . . As I was quietly sitting here minding my own business writing to you, this monk just asked me to marry him. At first I didn't understand. Anything vaguely romantic is so far from the tone of our strictly partnership relationship as to be inconceivable. The Japanese language allows sufficient ambiguity that at first I thought he was talking in the abstract, i.e., would I ever marry someone? I answered with what I thought was appropriate indifference, and by thus not initially refusing outright, I got a whole plot laid before me. He says that Go Roshi had said, if I wanted to marry this monk, it would be fine by him. He presented the proposal, if it could be called that, very practically. As he was sick, he needed a cook and we could continue life pretty much as before. My God, are they businesslike! I was almost too shocked to speak. He offered to support you and any of the kids here and said I could go back to Ireland every so often. I was still speechless and bumbled and stumbled and said I'd write to you. Meanwhile, Go Roshi had told me that he wanted me back in Tokyo, where I could train better with him. He had apologized profusely that I had to mind an 'invalid' and promised that by July at the latest I'd be back in Tokyo. He said that if I stayed for the 3 years' course of study (I'm half-way) that then I could go back to Ireland and teach. (I know he'd help finance a dojo.)

I made a lot of progress at this last sesshin (just got back). The monk who was translating for me said that in three days I did as many koans as he in six months! Go Roshi and I work well together and it would be difficult to find someone as good. So here are my options – give me your advice. In the midst of my stumblings with Tetsugen-san, and after he'd said 'Well then, it's decided. Let's marry' (At times like that my Japanese seems faulty. What had I said?), I, frantically searching for an out, said there was a boyfriend I still hadn't given up on and wanted to write to. I really hate this constant pressure to marry. Everyone worries that I'm getting old, etc. – it's only meant as kindness. But what I might do is accept this nebulous boyfriend, stay until the end of autumn (that will be two years), then go to France, find another Roshi, and do post-grad work.

The other option is to calm down (I am inclined to bolt terribly when people begin talking about marriage), then go back to Tokyo, finish my term of study properly, i.e., the three years, and get the whole training solidly under my belt. I do risk messing things up by breaking too soon. What do you think? Actually, having written to you I already feel calmer. Big deal – if everybody keeps pushing me to marry I can just refuse. I just get to squirming as if there's a noose there. Tetsugen will get over it; it's not as though he's in love with me or anything. But anyway, what do you think I should do? Try to be objective – not just thinking another year-and-a-half off in Japan, but thinking also about my qualifications for the future. Tell Nana not to worry. There's absolutely no way I'll stay in Japan. Cripes, at this rate they'll drive me out!

Anyway, sorry to have gone on at such length, but he just now sprang it on me. As I said, I'm just back from sesshin in Tokyo. It was excellent; I'd say the best one yet. Toshoji has changed a bit from my days there. Someone found out about the cheap dormitory accommodation they offer to Zen students and advertised it in an English paper so now there are four foreigners, even one woman. It's much less isolating, I should think, than before. One of the foreigners, a Jewish student from Pittsburgh called Paul is over here doing research on Japanese theatre. He got free tickets for a recital, so I went along. It was fantastic, and the best part was having a guide who could explain the various styles, techniques, and meanings of different gestures. It was called a dance recital, but they also did many pieces from Kabuki and Noh plays. They're marathon performances, starting at 12 noon and going on into the night. People drift in and out when they please. The pieces are unrelated, so they don't miss anything. The audience chats, shouts encouragement, picnics, and generally relaxes, having a good time. Watching them all decked out in magnificent, special occasion kimonos was almost as entertaining as the performance.

The other highlight of my Tokyo sojourn was going to Tessansan's marriage ceremony. It was my first wedding here and unusual in being Buddhist. Weddings are usually Shinto. They had only met a couple of times before the wedding, yet both were cool as cucumbers about it. She looked gorgeous, serene and radiant, as she sat waiting on a throne. Her head was covered by a white hood in deference to the superstition that women have horns! Her first outfit was white silk; then she changed several times, the number of changes being an indication of the wealth of the family. Poor girl, though – she had so many layers on she could scarcely move and couldn't touch a bite of her dinner. There's another custom which says that no one may mention parting, good-bye, or separation during the day. If they do, it's meant to bring bad luck, and the couple may split up. So everyone drifts away without good-byes.

The actual ceremony is very simple and beautiful (no promises of love!) They used a lacquer set just like yours to serve the bride and groom during the ceremony. Then, with sake poured from exquisitely ornamented gold vessels, we all drank to their health and prosperity. After the ceremony, a lot of sake flowed with a feast that made our weddings look like Saturday night's reheated leftovers. It was sumptuous (cost about $80.00 a head), and they even weighed us each down with presents as we left. As they were getting ready to go off to Kyushu on their honeymoon, they looked a funny pair. He wore western clothes instead of his monk's outfit. Having no hair with his navy-blue suit made him look a bit like a con-man: she with her tight, prim little suit could easily have been the social worker turned warden. We all went as far as Tokyo on the train together. The newlyweds sat in separate compartments without even a pretense of romance. Thank God I'm not Japanese.

So now I'm back here at Kannonji. I've just been out digging my vegetable patch, and there's great satisfaction in getting all the preparations done. I've calmed down a bit since my proposal. I'm sure Go Roshi did not suggest it, which is the impression Tetsugen-san was trying to give. Go Roshi always says he wants me back in Tokyo, where I can train more intensively. . . . See you soon.

Much much love,

M

Maura 'Soshin' O'Halloran, *Pure Heart and Enlightened Mind – The Zen Journal and Letters of an Irish Woman in Japan*, Thorsons, HarperCollins, London (1995)

APPENDIX:
EPISTOLARY NOVELS

There is little sign of the epistolary novel as a major genre in Irish literature. The only Irish woman to have made a notable contribution in this field was the remarkable Maria Edgeworth. Two examples of her work in this fashion are Leonora *and* Letters of Julia and Caroline, *both published in 1848. The letters chosen from these works both deal with marriage – an experience Maria herself never underwent. Possibly the content of these 'imaginary' letters shows why.*

DISILLUSION WITH MARRIAGE

This is an imaginary letter from a work called Leonora, *published in 1848, consisting of an interchange of letters between the imaginary Lady Olivia and Lady Leonora; this letter reveals the disillusion felt by Lady Olivia on discovering that hers was not a marriage between two minds. It is a remarkable composition for a lady from the Irish midlands – but then Maria Edgeworth was a remarkable woman.*

OLIVIA TO LEONORA

Full of life and spirits, with a heart formed for all the enthusiasm, for all the delicacy of love, I married early, in the fond expectation of meeting a heart suited to my own. Cruelly disappointed, I found – merely a husband. My heart recoiled upon itself; true to my own principles of virtue, I scorned dissimulation. I candidly confessed to my husband, that my love was extinguished. I proved to him, alas! too clearly, that we were not born for each other. The attractive moment of illusion was past – never more to return; the repulsive reality remained. The living was chained to the dead, and, by the inexorable tyranny of English laws, that chain, eternally galling to innocence, can be severed only by the desperation of vice. Divorce, according to our barbarous institutions, cannot be obtained without guilt. Appalled at the thought, I saw no hope but in submission. Yet to submit to live with the man I could not love was, to a mind like mine, impossible. My principles and my feelings equally revolted from this legal prostitution. We separated. I sought for balm to my wounded heart in foreign climes.

To the beauties of nature I was ever feelingly alive. Amidst the sublime scenes of Switzerland, and on the consecrated borders of her classic lakes, I sometimes forgot myself to happiness. Felicity, how transient! – transient as the day-dreams that played upon my fancy in the bright morning of love. Alas! not all creation's charms could soothe me to repose. I wandered in search of that which change of place cannot afford. There was an aching void in my heart – an indescribable sadness over my spirits. Sometimes I had recourse to books; but how few were in unison with my feelings, or touched the trembling chords of my disordered mind! Commonplace morality I could not endure. History presented nothing but a mass of crimes. Metaphysics promised some relief, and I bewildered myself in their not inelegant labyrinth. But to the bold genius and exquisite pathos of some German novelists I hold myself indebted for my largest portion of ideal bliss; for those rapt moments, when sympathy with kindred souls transported me into better worlds, and consigned vulgar realities to oblivion.

I am well aware, my Leonora, that you approve not of these my favourite writers: but yours is the morality of one who has never known sorrow. I also would interdict such cordials to the happy. But would you forbid those to taste felicity in dreams who feel any misery when awake? Would you dash the cup of Lethe from lips to which no other beverage is salubrious or sweet?

By the use of these opiates my soul gradually settled into a sort of pleasing pensive melancholy. Has it not been said, that melancholy is a characteristic of genius? I make no pretensions to genius: but I am persuaded that melancholy is the habitual, perhaps the natural state of those who have the misfortune to feel with delicacy.

You, my dear Leonora, will class this notion amongst what you once called my refined errors. Indeed I must confess, that I see in you an exception so striking as almost to compel me to relinquish my theory. But again let me remind you, that your lot in life has been different from mine. Alas! how different! Why had not I such a friend, such a mother as yours, early to direct my uncertain steps, and to educate me to happiness? I might have been – But no matter what I might have been – I must tell you what I have been.

Separated from my husband, without a guide, without a friend at the most perilous period of my life, I was left to that most insidious of counsellors – my own heart – my own weak heart. When I was least prepared to resist the impression, it was my misfortune to meet with a man of a soul congenial with my own. Before I felt my danger, I was entangled beyond the possibility of escape. The net was thrown over my heart; its struggles were to no purpose but to exhaust my strength. Virtue commanded me to be miserable – and I was miserable. But do I dare to expect your pity, Leonora, for such an attachment? It excites your indignation, perhaps your horror. Blame, despise, detest me; all this would I rather bear, than deceive you into fancying me better than I really am.

Do not, however, think me worse. If my views had been less pure, if I had felt less reliance on the firmness of my own principles, and less repugnance to artifice, I might easily have avoided some appearances, which have injured me in the eyes of the world. With real contrition I confess, that a fatal mixture of masculine independence of spirit, and of female tenderness of heart, has betrayed me into many imprudences; but of vice, and of that meanest species of vice, hypocrisy, I thank Heaven, my conscience can acquit me. All I have now to hope is, that you, my indulgent, my generous Leonora, will not utterly condemn me. Truth and gratitude are my only claims to your friendship – to a friendship, which would be to me the first of earthly blessings, which might make me amends for all I have lost. Consider this before, unworthy as I am, you reject me from your esteem, Counsel, guide, save me! Without vanity, but with confidence I say it, I have a heart that will repay you for affection. You will find me easily moved, easily governed by kindness. Yours has already sunk deep into my soul, and your power is unlimited over the affections and over the understanding of

Your obliged

Olivia

Maria Edgeworth, *Leonora*, Simpkin, Marshall and Co., London (1848)

ON HER INTENDED MARRIAGE

This is another literary letter, from an epistolary novel Letters of Julia and Caroline, *published in 1848, written by the imaginary Caroline to her friend Julia, assessing the merits (and demerits) of the intended marriage with sensitivity.*

CAROLINE TO JULIA
On her intended marriage

Indeed, my dear Julia, I hardly know how to venture to give you my advice upon a subject which ought to depend so much upon your own taste and feelings. My opinion and my wishes I could readily tell you: the idea of seeing you united and attached to my brother is certainly the most agreeable to me; but I am to divest myself of the partiality of a sister, and to consider my brother and Lord V—— as equal candidates for your preference – equal, I mean, in your regard; for you say that 'Your heart is not yet decided in its choice, – If that oracle would declare itself in intelligible terms, you would not hesitate a moment to obey its dictates.' But, my dear Julia, is there not another, a *safer*, I do not say a *better* oracle, to be consulted – your reason? Whilst the 'doubtful beam still nods from side to side,' you may with a steady hand weigh your own motives, and determine what things will be essential to your happiness, and what *price* you will pay for them; for

> Each pleasure has its *price*; and they who pay
> Too much of pain, but squander life away.

Do me the justice to believe that I do not quote these lines of Dryden as being the finest poetry he ever wrote; for poets, you know, as Waller wittily observed, never succeed so well in truth as in fiction.

Since we cannot in life expect to realize all our wishes, we must distinguish those which claim the rank of wants. We must separate the fanciful from the real, or at least make the one subservient to the other.

It is of the utmost importance to you, more particularly, to take every precaution before you decide for life, because disappointment and restraint afterwards would be insupportable to your temper.

You have often declared to me, my dear friend, that your love of poetry, and of all the refinements of literary and romantic pursuits, is so intimately 'interwoven in your mind, that nothing could separate them, without destroying the whole fabric.'

Your tastes, you say, are fixed; if they are so, you must be doubly careful to ensure their gratification. If you cannot make *them* subservient to external circumstances, you should certainly, if it be in your power, choose a situation in which circumstances will be subservient to them. If you are convinced that you could not adopt the tastes of another, it will be absolutely necessary for your happiness to live with one whose tastes are similar to your own.

The belief in that sympathy of souls, which the poets suppose declares itself between two people at first sight, is perhaps as absurd as the late fashionable belief in animal magnetism: but there is a sympathy which, if it be not the foundation, may be called the cement of affection. Two people could not, I should think, retain any lasting affection for each other, without a mutual sympathy in taste and in their diurnal occupations and domestic pleasures. This, you will allow, my dear Julia, even in a fuller extent than I do. Now, my brother's tastes, character, and habits of life, are so very different from Lord V——'s, that I scarcely know how you can compare them; at least before you can decide which of the two would make you the happiest in life; you must determine what kind of life you may wish to lead; for my brother, though he might make you very happy in domestic life, would not make the Countess of V—— happy; nor would Lord V—— make Mrs. Percy happy. They must be two different women, with different habits, and different wishes; so that you must divide yourself, my dear Julia, like Araspes, into two selves; I do not say into a bad and a good self; choose some other epithets to distinguish them, but distinct they must be: so let them now declare and decide their pretensions; and let the victor have not only the honours of a triumph, but all the prerogatives of victory. Let the subdued be subdued for life – let the victor take every precaution which policy can dictate, to prevent the possibility of future contests with the vanquished.

But without talking poetry to you, my dear friend, let me seriously recommend it to you to examine your own mind carefully; and if you find that public diversions and public admiration, dissipation, and all the pleasures of riches and high rank, are really and truly essential to your happiness, direct your choice accordingly. Marry Lord V——: he has a large fortune, extensive connexions, and an exalted station; his own taste for show and expense, his family pride, and personal vanity, will all tend to the end you propose. Your house, table, equipages, may be all in the highest style of magnificence, Lord V——'s easiness of temper, and fondness for you, will readily give you the entire ascendancy over his pleasures, which your abilities give you over his understanding. He will not control your wishes; you may gratify them to the utmost bounds of his fortune, and perhaps beyond those bounds; you may have entire command at home and abroad. If these are your objects, Julia, take them; they are in your power. But remember, you must take them with their necessary concomitants – the restraints upon your time, upon the choice of your friends and your company, which high life imposes; the *ennui* subsequent to dissipation; the mortifications of rivalship in beauty, wit, rank, and magnificence; the trouble of managing a large fortune, and the chance of involving your affairs and your family in difficulty and distress; these and a thousand more evils you must submit to. You must renounce all the pleasures of the heart and of the imagination; you must give up the idea of cultivating literary taste; you must not expect from your husband friendship and confidence, or any of the delicacies of affection; – you govern him, he cannot therefore be your equal; you may be a fond mother, but you cannot educate your children; you will neither have the time nor the power to do it; you must trust them to a governess. In the selection of your friends, and in the enjoyment of their company and conversation, you will be still more restrained: in short, you must give up the pleasures of domestic life; for that is not in this case the life you have chosen. But you will exclaim against me for supposing you capable of making such a choice – such sacrifices! – I am sure, *next to my brother*, I am the last person in the world who would wish you to make them.

You have another choice, my dear Julia: domestic life is offered to you by one who has every wish and every power to make it agreeable to you; by one whose tastes resemble your own; who would be a judge and a fond admirer of all your perfections. You would have perpetual motives to cultivate every talent, and to exert every power of pleasing for his sake – for *his* sake, whose penetration no improvement would escape, and whose affection would be susceptible of every proof of yours. Am I drawing too flattering a picture? – A sister's hand may draw a partial likeness, but still it will be a likeness. At all events, my dear Julia, you would be certain of the mode of life you would lead with my brother. The regulation of your time and occupations would be your own. In the education of your family, you would meet with no interruptions or restraint. You would have no governess to counteract, no strangers to intrude; you might follow your own judgment, or yield to the judgment of one who would never require you to submit to his opinion, but to his reasons.

All the pleasures of friendship you would enjoy in your own family in the highest perfection, and you would have for your sister the friend of your infancy,

Caroline

Maria Edgeworth, *Letters of Julia and Caroline*,
Simpkin Marshall and Co., London (1848)

SELECTED ANCILLARY BIOGRAPHIES

Brontë, Patrick (Revd) (1777–1861): Brontë was born at Drumballyroney, near Loughbrickland, Co. Down. The original form of the family name was 'Prunty' or 'O'Prunty' (Irish Ó Pronntaigh). He became a blacksmith in a linen-mill, but taught and tutored the children of Revd Tighe, Rector of Drumgooland, with whose encouragement and assistance he went to St John's College, Cambridge, and was ordained in 1806. After curacies in Essex and Yorkshire he became perpetual curate in Haworth. His three daughters, Charlotte, Emily and Anne, all of whom he outlived, secured lasting literary fame for the family.

Burghley, William Cecil, Lord (1521–98): Burghley was born in Lincolnshire and was educated for the legal profession. Queen Elizabeth recognized his ability and appointed him Chief Secretary of State, an office he held for forty years, until his death. He was made a baron in 1571 and in 1572 succeeded the Marquess of Winchester as Lord High Treasurer.

Colgan, John (?1592–1658): Colgan was born in Co. Donegal and around 1618 joined the Franciscan Order in Louvain. Here he later became involved in the enormous task of editing and annotating the collections of manuscripts assembled in Louvain pertaining to the ecclesiastical history of Ireland. In 1645 he published a large volume on the Lives of the Irish Saints, to be followed in 1647 by another large volume covering the Lives of Saints Patrick, Brigid and Colmcille. Unfortunately, many of the manuscripts used in these publications, and others relating to unpublished works, have disappeared.

Collins, Mícheál (1890–1922): Collins was born in Clonakilty, Co. Cork. While working in an office in London he joined the Irish Republican Brotherhood and, after fighting in the Easter Rising of 1916, was interned. In 1917 he met Catherine (Kitty) Kiernan, while he was assisting Joseph McGuiness in a by-election in Co. Longford. He was a minister in the Dáil executive and Director of Intelligence for the Irish Republican Army. In the Irish Civil War he commanded the forces of the Irish Free State and was killed in an ambush at Béal na Bláth, Co. Cork.

Joyce, James Augustine Aloysius (1882–1941): Joyce was born in Rathgar, Dublin, the son of a middle-class Catholic. As a result of the depletion of his father's finances his education, starting at Clongowes Wood, in 1888, was reduced to attending Belvedere College as a non-paying student. In 1895 he entered the Royal University on a scholarship to study languages. Even at this stage Joyce described himself as a poet and an artist. In 1902 the problem of earning a living led him to opt for medicine and he enrolled in the medical school of the Royal University in 1902, but left for Paris with the idea of training there instead, only to be frustrated by difficulties over entrance qualifications. In 1904 he met Nora Barnacle with whom he eloped to the continent, to live a rather nomadic life – supporting himself and his wife and family mainly by teaching English. His published literary career really began in 1914 with the publication of *Dubliners*, to be followed in 1916 by *A Portrait of the Artist as a Young Man*. *Ulysses* appeared in time for his fortieth birthday in 1922. It was 1939 before *Finnegan's Wake* appeared.

McCracken, Henry Joy (1767–98): McCracken was born in Belfast of well-to-do parents. By the age of twenty-two he was the owner of a successful cotton factory. He was a founding member of the United Irishmen and in 1767 was arrested and imprisoned in Kilmainham Jail, Dublin. He was released a year later. In the rebellion of 1798 he was commander of the forces at Antrim; his forces were routed and he escaped to the mountains with the remainder of his men. He attempted to escape to America but was recognized and arrested. After a court martial he was convicted of treason, but refused an offer of clemency in return for informing on his fellows. He was publicly hanged in Belfast in July 1798.

Russell, Thomas (1787–1803): Russell was born in Betsborough, Co. Cork, the son of an officer in the British army, who was subsequently appointed to a position in the Royal Hospital, Kilmainham. Like his father Thomas, he was originally intended for the church, but, again like his father, joined the army instead. In 1789 he met Theobald Wolfe Tone and in 1791 his regiment was stationed in Belfast. He made the acquaintance of many of the leading liberal politicians in the town, including Samuel Neilson and Henry Joy McCracken. He was obliged to sell his commission but was appointed Seneschal of the Manor Court of Dungannon and a JP for Co. Tyrone – offices which he later felt irreconcilable with the concept of liberal democracy.

In 1792 he returned to Belfast and devoted himself increasingly to the principles of the United Irishmen. His friendship with Henry Joy McCracken and his sister, Mary Ann, prospered. In 1796 he was arrested in Belfast and held in close confinement in Dublin until 1799. On his release he escaped to the continent, where he became involved with Robert Emmet. On his return to Ireland in disguise he was recognized, arrested and removed to Kilmainham Jail. An unsuccessful attempt was made by Mary Ann McCracken to bribe his jailor. He was moved to Downpatrick where he was tried, sentenced and executed.

Shaw, George Bernard (1856–1950): Shaw was born in Dublin and was first employed as a clerk in an estate-management firm before moving to London in 1876. His first literary efforts written during the period 1879–83, were five novels, which were rejected by English publishers, although four of them were published serially. In 1884 he joined the Fabian Society, which deepened his association with Sidney and Beatrice Webb. He made his debut as a playwright in 1892 when *Widowers'*

Houses was produced at the Royalty Theatre. By 1896 the seven plays grouped together as 'Plays Pleasant and Unpleasant' had been completed. In 1898 he married Charlotte Payne-Townshend – a marriage that by mutual agreement was 'companionate'. This marriage endured until Charlotte's death in 1943. His career as a playwright, with works such as *Man and Superman* (1905), *The Doctor's Dilemma* (1906) and *Saint Joan* (1923), was crowned in 1925 when he was awarded the Nobel Prize for Literature.

Southey, Robert (1774–1843): Southey was born in Bristol and after being expelled from Westminster School went up to Balliol College, Oxford, where he stayed for one year. In 1795 he clandestinely married Edith Fricker, a sister of Mrs Coleridge. He visited his uncle in Lisbon and in six months laid the foundations of his knowledge of Spanish history and literature. He settled in Keswick, where he devoted himself to writing, and after the publication of *Joan of Arc*, *Thalaba*, *Madoc* and *The Curse of Kehama* he was made Poet Laureate in 1813.

Wilde, Oscar Fingal O'Flahertie Wills (1854–1900): Oscar Wilde was born in Dublin, the second son of Sir William Wilde and Lady Jane Wilde. He was educated at Portora Royal School, Enniskillen, Co. Fermanagh, Trinity College, Dublin, and Magdalen College, Oxford. In 1884 he married Constance Lloyd, with whom he had two children, Cyril and Vyvyan. His literary success began in 1890, when his only novel, *The Picture of Dorian Gray*, was published. In 1886 he had begun to have sexual relationships with men, first Robert Ross and then in 1891 Lord Alfred Douglas. In 1895 his *An Ideal Husband* and *The Importance of being Earnest* were produced. Meanwhile his relationship with Douglas continued, until the Marquess of Queensbury (Douglas's father) lured him into taking an action for criminal libel. He was forced to abandon the action and in turn was himself charged with gross indecency. He was convicted and sentenced to two years penal servitude with hard labour. On his release from Reading Gaol he left England bankrupt and homeless and drifted round Europe until his death in Paris in 1900.

Wilde, Sir William Robert Wills (1815–76): Sir William Wilde was born in Castlerea, Co. Roscommon. After leaving the Royal College of Surgeons in Dublin, he was engaged as a personal physician, and wrote *A Narrative of a Voyage to Madeira, Teneriffe, etc.* As a result of its success he was able to pursue his studies in London, Berlin and Vienna before settling in Dublin and setting up as an eye and ear consultant. In 1851 he married Jane Francesca Elgee, with whom he had two sons, the second of whom was Oscar, and one daughter. He compiled an important and pioneering catalogue of archaeological material in the collections of the Royal Irish Academy, published in 1862. In 1864, the year of the Mary Travers scandal, he was knighted.

Yeats, William Butler (1865–1939): W.B. Yeats was born in Dublin, the son of John Butler Yeats, a painter. His mother, Susan Pollexfen, came from a well-to-do family in Co. Sligo. His early life alternated between London and Sligo until, in 1881, the family returned to Ireland. In 1884 he entered the Metropolitan School of Art, where he met George Russell. In 1888 he wrote what is probably his best-known poem, 'The Lake Isle of Innisfree'. The following year *The Wanderings of Oisin* was published; this was also the year in which he met Maud Gonne, a beautiful young woman of independent means, with whom he promptly fell in love and for whom, in 1892, he wrote his play *The Countess Cathleen*. She rejected his first proposal of marriage in 1891, and many subsequent ones. In 1893 he published *The Celtic Twilight* – the title of which gave its name to the kind of dreamy romantic poetry much in vogue at the time. He had first met Lady Gregory in London in 1894, and in 1896 visited her at Coole Park, Co. Galway. With her and Edward Martyn he planned the Irish Literary Theatre. Having been finally turned down by Maud Gonne he married Georgie Hyde Lees in 1917. In 1923 he was awarded the Nobel Prize for Literature.

FURTHER READING

If you want to read more letters by Irish women, the sources mentioned in the acknowledgements should prove fruitful. If, on the other hand, you want a general study of women and letter-writing, and of the development of means of conveying letters from the writer to the recipient then the introduction to *800 Years of Women's Letters*, compiled by Olga Kenyon (Sutton Publishing, Stroud, 1992) contains a superb account of the mechanisms; the body of the book contains a grand selection of international women's letters.

If, alternatively, you want more information about Irish history, you have many choices: you can opt for a speedy crash-course by resorting to the excellent *Short History of Ireland*, by Richard Killeen (Gill and Macmillan, Dublin, 1995) or, of course, you can devote many avid hours to *A New History of Ireland*, ultimately consisting of nine volumes, under the editorships of T.W. Moody, F.X. Martin and F.J. Byrne (Oxford, 1976).

If all you want is a little help with Irish literature then help is conveniently at hand in the form of *The Oxford Companion to Irish Literature*, which encompasses all aspects of Irish Literature – whether in Latin, Irish or English.

Finally – if what you really want is a highlight on Irish women's writings – there is *Ireland's Women – Writings Past and Present*, edited by Katie Donovan, A. Norman Jeffares and Brendan Kennelly (Gill and Macmillan, Dublin, 1994).

ACKNOWLEDGEMENTS

The compiler and publisher wish to record their thanks for permission to include letters by the following writers:

Brontë, Anne, Brontë, Charlotte and Brontë, Emily: in *The Brontë Letters*, compiled by Muriel Spark, Peter Nevill

Brontë, Charlotte: in *The Brontës: Their Lives, Friendships and Correspondence in Four Volumes*, edited by T.J. Wise and J.A. Symington, Oxford University Press

Burke, Biddy, Dalton, Eliza and Wyly, Isabella: in *Oceans of Consolation: Personal Accounts of Irish Migration to Australia*, edited by David Fitzpatrick, Cork University Press

Darragh, Florence and Yeats, Lily: in *Letters to W.B. Yeats*, edited by Richard J. Finneran, George Mills Harper and William M. Murphy, Macmillan

Delany, Mary: in *Letters from Georgian Ireland: the Correspondence of Mary Delany, 1731–1768*, The Friar's Bush Press

Edgeworth, Maria: in *Maria Edgeworth: Letters from England, 1813–1844*, edited by Christina Colvin, Oxford University Press

Joyce, Nora: in *Nora: a Biography of Nora Joyce*, by Brenda Maddox, Hamish Hamilton

Kiernan, Kitty: in *In Great Haste: the Letters of Michael Collins and Kitty Kiernan*, edited by León Ó Broin, Gill and Macmillan

MacBride, Maud Gonne: in *The Gonne–Yeats Letters 1893–1938*, edited by Anna MacBride White and A. Norman Jeffares, Hutchinson

McCracken, Ann and McCracken, Mary Ann: in *The Life and Times of Mary Ann McCracken*, by Mary McNeill, Blackstaff Press

Markievicz, Constance: in *Prison Letters of Countess Markievicz*, edited by Esther Roper, Virago Press

Martin, Violet and Somerville, Edith: in *The Selected Letters of Somerville and Ross*, edited by Gifford Lewis, Faber and Faber

O'Halloran, Maura ('Soshin'): in *Pure Heart, Enlightened Mind*, Thorsons/HarperCollins (by permission of Charles E. Tuttle Co., Inc.)

Shaw, Charlotte Frances: in *Mrs G.B.S. – A Biographical Portrait of Charlotte Shaw*, by Janet Dunbar, George G. Harrap and Co.

Wilde, Constance: in *Mrs Oscar Wilde: A Woman of Some Importance*, by Anne Clark Amor, Sidgwick and Jackson

Wilde, Lady Jane: in *The Parents of Oscar Wilde: Sir William and Lady Wilde*, by Terence de Vere White, Hodder and Stoughton

Every effort has been made to contact every source and, where replies have not been received, profound apologies are offered if the source cited is not correct.

INDEX